Dea

W

M

and happy reading....

love

Sara, Dan, Esme & Tau

x x x x

Two-Seat Spitfires

THE COMPLETE STORY

Greg Davis, John Sanderson and Peter Arnold

In association with
The Two-Seat Spitfire Page
on Facebook

Front cover: Superb formation of the three *Biggin Hill Heritage Hangar*-operated Spitfire Trainers, namely MJ772 leading MJ627 and unique Mk.VIII Prototype MT818. *(Image: Richard Paver)*

Back cover: *Aero Legends* NH341 with single-seat stablemate TD314 over the Kent countryside during the summer of 2017. *(Image: Richard Paver)*

Matt Jones sitting on the wing of the *Silver Spitfire*, single-seat Mk.IX MJ271, during the epic round the world trip undertaken in 2019. *(Image: Benjamin Uttley / Stamp Productions via Matt Jones)*

FOREWORD

I am delighted to write this foreword for *Two-Seat Spitfires: The Complete Story*. The Spitfire holds an incredibly special place in the hearts and psyche of people, not only in the UK but also across the world.

In 2019, I circumnavigated the world in *'The Silver Spitfire - The Longest Flight'* and wherever we travelled on our 27,000-mile journey we were greeted with such passion and excitement. The Spitfire captures hearts like no other aircraft!

I have had the privilege of flying many people in two-seat Spitfires over the years. Every one of them has an intense reaction to flying in this most iconic aircraft. Some of the passengers are so excited that they can barely put what they are feeling into words, others are moved literally to tears. Flying in a two-seat Spitfire is one of the most exhilarating and wonderful things to do.

Greg, John, and Peter fully understand the thrill and excitement that flying in these aircraft engenders and this has driven them to write this wonderful and fascinating book.

This book has been a labour of love and they have combined to produce what is without doubt the most complete overview of the two-seat Spitfires yet written. This book explains the background to the aircraft, their histories, where you can fly in them and what it really feels like to fulfil that dream.

I commend this book to you as an appreciation of everything to do with *The Two-Seat Spitfires*.

Matt Jones
Spitfire Pilot and Instructor

INTRODUCTION

The Spitfire. There have been many hundreds, maybe even thousands, of books written about this beautiful, R.J. Mitchell designed, elliptically winged aeroplane. But there has yet to be a book published which has focussed solely on the lesser-known two-seat variant of the graceful Spitfire - until now…

The genesis of this book came about in 2016 when Greg Davis took a flight in Spitfire Trainer MJ627, operated by Biggin Hill Heritage Hangar. Little did he know when flying over the Kentish countryside that it would be the start of something bigger. This flight began an interest in all things two-seat Spitfire related, and when he launched The Two-Seat Spitfire Page on Facebook it became the 'go to' place for the topic. Greg produced a small 50-page book on the subject. Whilst it was well received Greg was already making plans for a greatly expanded version.

Greg approached John Sanderson, a well-known Spitfire historian, to join him to expand the book and provide a much more detailed study of the two-seat Spitfire. With work on the book fully underway, the decision was made to invite Peter Arnold, world-renowned Spitfire expert and co-author of the definitive Spitfire Survivors books, to come onboard as the third co-author. The assembled team, along with their amassed knowledge and experience, was now in place to produce the most comprehensive work on the topic ever published.

The goal was to produce the definitive work on the history of the Spitfire Trainer from inception through to the present day, and we believe this has been achieved.

In this year of the 80th Anniversary of the Battle of Britain, we cannot help but remember the brave 'Few' who flew the single-seat version of these amazing machines all those years ago and to whom we, and indeed the whole world, owe our heartfelt gratitude. One cannot fly in, or even sit in, a Spitfire without remembering their sacrifice. We hope that, in reading this book, you will be inspired to make the effort to see, sit in, or maybe even fly in one of these majestic and rare aeroplanes.

Please note that whilst every effort has been made to accurately credit all the included images to their respective original photographer, due to the age of many of them this has not been possible. In these cases, the images are attributed to the collection from whence they came.

If, as you read the book, you realise that you have some information, or even an interesting anecdote relating to the two-seat Spitfire which we have not included, then please feel free to contact us so that we can include it in future editions.

Greg Davis, John Sanderson and Peter Arnold
July 2020

For book feedback please visit
www.TwoSeatSpitfires.com

For up to date Two-Seat Spitfire news please visit
www.facebook.com/TheTwoSeatSpitfirePage

A wonderful Spitfire Trainer formation over the Kent countryside organised by *Aero Legends* during 2019, with NH341 leading PV202 and SM520. *(Image: Richard Paver)*

ACKNOWLEDGEMENTS

As with any book there are always many people to thank, and this one is no exception.

Firstly, the authors must thank the many contributors who have generously provided information or photographs for inclusion in the book, we are extremely grateful.

Our sincere thanks go to: Roger Barrett, Jeff Carless, Gavin Conroy, Dr. Martin Davis, Herman Dekker, Mike Edwards, Jason Elmore, Stuart Gennery, Benjamin Gilbert, Peter Green, Darren Harbar, Nigel Harrison, Matt Jones, Tony Kearns, Oleg Korytov, Dean Large, Bob Levens, Wojtek Matusiak, Nicholas McIndoe, Paul McMillan, Xavier Meal, Harry Measures, Chris Michell, Alex Monk, Peter Monk, Fred Mussard, Ross Pay, Keith Perkins, Jagan Pillarisetti, Col Pope, Jerry Ridout, Mark Rutley, Will Samuelson, R A. Scholefield, Ady Shaw, Graham Skillen, Gerry Sturgess, Jean-Pierre Touzeau, Harry Van Der Meer, Runar Vassbotten, Steve Vizard, Stewart Waring, and Malcolm R Wells.

An incredibly special thank you goes to Richard Paver, the aerial photography consultant for this book. He has allowed so many of his stunning air-to-air images of surviving Spitfire Trainers to be included, as well providing an insight of how he captures them. Thank you, Richard.

A huge thank you is also due to Bertrand Brown for his superb aircraft profiles created exclusively for the book. The attention to detail is just wonderful.

A special thank you to both Jo Rogers and Roger Barrett for their expert proof-reading skills, much appreciated.

Gratitude must go out to the staff and volunteers of the following organisations for their support: Aero Legends, Air Leasing, Aircraft Restoration Company, Airframe Assemblies Ltd, Biggin Hill Heritage Hangar, Boultbee Flight Academy, Classic Wings, Historic Flying Ltd, Norwegian Flying Aces, The Spitfire Company (Biggin Hill), and Warbird Adventure Rides Ltd.

CONTENTS

THE TWO-SEAT SPITFIRE LIST

(Aircraft listed in bold are extant at the time of writing)

Mk.VIII Trainer – Vickers Armstrongs Ltd. Factory Conversions

RAF Serial	Civil Reg.	Previous Identities & Notes
MT818	G-AIDN	Construction no. 6S/729058 N32, N58JE, N818MT
Serial unknown	G-AKBD	Construction no. 6S/730847 Conversion not carried out. Struck off civilian register 31 May 1948.

Mk.IX Trainer – Vickers Armstrongs Ltd. Factory Conversions

Netherlands

BS147	--	G.15-1, H-99, 3W-22, PH-NFN
BS274	--	N-42, H-98, 3W-20, 'BF274'
MK715	--	N-41, H-97, 3W-21

Egypt

ML113	G-ALJM	G.15-92, Royal Egyptian Air Force No.684.
Serial unknown	--	Potential additional aircraft, not confirmed.

India

MA848	--	G.15-2, HS534/90
MH432	--	G.15-3, HS535/81
MJ177	--	G.15-4, HS536
MJ276	--	G.15-5, HS537
MJ451	--	G.15-6, HS538
MJ518	--	G.15-7, HS539/A
MK172	--	G.15-8, HS540
MK176	--	G.15-9, HS541
MK298	--	G.15-10, HS542
ML417	N2TF	G.15-11, HS543, G-BJSG Reverted to single-seat configuration.

Ireland

MJ627	G-BMSB	G.15-171, IAC No.158, G-ASOZ
MJ772	G-AVAV	G.15-172, IAC No.159, N8R, D-FMKN
MK721	--	G.15-173, IAC No.160
ML407	G-LFIX	G.15-175, IAC No.162
PV202	G-CCCA	G.15-174, IAC No.161, G-BHGH, G-TRIX, 'H-98', 'AI-E', 'QV-I'
TE308	G-AWGB	G.15-176, IAC No.163, CF-RAF, C-FRAF, N92477, N308WK

Orders Cancelled & Enquiries

Country	Notes
Argentina	Argentine Air Force order for ten (10) Mk.IX Trainer aircraft cancelled in the 1950s. Purchased Fiat G.55B instead.
India	Indian Air Force understood they would be receiving four (4) Mk.XVIII two-seat Trainer aircraft within their second order for the type. Not confirmed, and none built or delivered.
Iraq	Iraqi Air Force order for six (6) Mk.IX Trainer aircraft cancelled in the 1950s.
Norway	Norwegian Air Force expressed interest to convert several existing Mk.IX aircraft to two-seat Trainer configuration. No agreement reached.

Conversions and Rebuilds

In-Service Conversions

RAF Serial	Notes
ES127	Mk.Vb Trop with additional cockpit in place of fuel-tank ahead of pilot. In-field conversion, Sicily, 1944.
MJ800	Mk.IX converted to include an additional cockpit behind the pilot. Converted in the Moscow area, May 1945
Serial unknown	Soviet Air Force converted further Mk.IX aircraft, potentially as many as fifty (50), to include an additional cockpit behind the pilot.

Warbird-Era Rebuilds

RAF Serial	Civil Reg.	Previous Identities & Notes
PT462	G-CTIX	Rebuilt in Trainer configuration. Flown 1987. Ex. MM4100, 20-67, 4X-FOM, N462JC
MH367	ZK-WDQ	Rebuilt in Trainer configuration. Flown 2006. Ex. N367MH
SM520	G-ILDA	Rebuilt in Trainer configuration. Flown 2008. Ex. G-BXHZ, 'H-99'
NH341	G-CICK	Rebuilt in Trainer configuration. Flown 2017.
BS410	G-TCHI	Under rebuild to Trainer configuration.
EN570	LN-AOA	Under rebuild to 'Grace-Melton' Trainer configuration. Ex. G-CISP
BS548	--	Under rebuild to 'Grace-Melton' Trainer configuration.
Serial withheld #1	--	Mk.IX Under rebuild to Trainer configuration.
Serial withheld #2	--	Mk.IX Under rebuild to Trainer configuration.
EN179	G-TCHO	Project. To be rebuilt in Trainer configuration.

Notes:

1. Listed in the order they were, or are being, rebuilt

2. Serial numbers in parentheses are spurious identities that have been carried

SPITFIRE TRAINER PROFILES

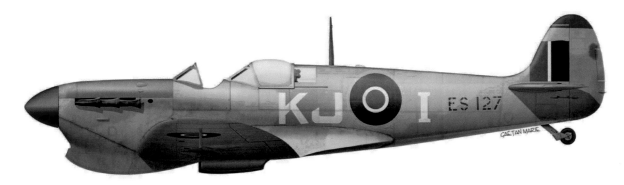

Spitfire Mk.V ES127, an ex 4 Sqn. South African Air Force aircraft modified in-service whilst in Sicily, 1944.

Soviet Air Force Spitfire Mk.IX (potentially MJ800), locally converted to two-seat UTI configuration, circa 1945.

Prototype Spitfire Trainer Mk.VIII MT818 wearing Class B markings *N32*, circa 1946.

Mk.IX BS274 / *'BF274'* in Royal Netherlands Air Force service as *H-98*, 1948.

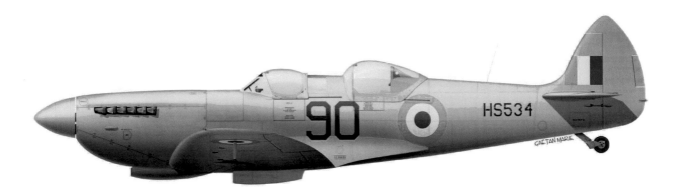

Mk.IX MA848 in Royal Indian Air Force service as *HS534*, circa November 1948.

Mk.IX ML407 wearing early all-over green scheme whilst in Irish Air Corps service as *162*, circa 1951.

Mk.IX BS147 (PH-NFN) when in service with Schreiner Aero Contractors, mid 1950s.

Mk.IX PV202 wearing later all-over silver scheme whilst in service with the Irish Air Corps as *161*, late 1950s.

(Profile drawings copyright Gaëtan Marie / www.bravobravoaviation.com)

NOT FACTORY BUILT

The Spitfire Trainer was not produced by Vickers-Armstrongs Ltd at their factories. There is no such thing as a *factory-built* Spitfire Trainer.

Every Spitfire Trainer aircraft that has ever existed was originally built at the factory as a single-seat airframe, and subsequently converted to include a second cockpit at a later date.

Each of the individual aircraft histories included within this book detail where the aircraft was built, as a single-seat airframe, and describes subsequent service and post-service history, including the conversion to Spitfire Trainer configuration.

THE EARLY AIRCRAFT

Whilst the first Vickers-Armstrongs Ltd Spitfire Trainer appeared during 1946, there were however some *unofficial* conversions before that date and in this chapter, we provide the albeit limited information of those early aircraft.

Soviet Air Force UTI

The British Government supplied the Soviet Union with over one thousand one hundred (1,100) Mk.IX Spitfires under the wartime Lend-Lease policy, with deliveries beginning in February 1944.

The Soviet Air Force (*Voyenno-Vozdushnye Sily*/VVS) expressed interest in the Spitfire Mk.IX Trainer variant, but this did not translate into an order for the Vickers-Armstrongs built conversions. However, and to address this interest, several of the Lend-Lease provided single-seat Spitfires were converted in Russia to include a second seat behind the pilot position.

As you will read later in the book, when Vickers-Armstrongs Ltd undertook conversion of single-seat aircraft to trainer configuration they moved the front cockpit forwards to accommodate the rear position. This was not the approach taken by the Soviet Union, where the front cockpit remained in the original position, meaning the rear cockpit was therefore further aft and in a narrower section of the fuselage. The rear cockpit appears to utilise a standard single-seat Spitfire blister canopy which, being slightly wider than the rear fuselage, results in a generous gap at the back. There are indications that Type RD-1 radar was fitted in the rear cockpit of these converted aircraft.

These converted aircraft were given the designation UTI (*Uchebno-Trenirovochnyy Istrebitel*/Training Fighter) in Soviet Air Force service.

Soviet Air Force Mk.IX following conversion to UTI status by 1ARB, Leningrad during summer 1945. *(Image: Peter Arnold Collection)*

Following research of the records held within the Central Archives of the Ministry of Defence of the Russian Federation (TsAMO) it has been possible to confirm the RAF serial number for one of the aircraft converted to UTI status. Delivered to the Soviet Air Force in mid-1944, Spitfire Mk.IX MJ800 was assigned to 16 IAP (Fighter Air Regiment). On 6 May 1945 she was dispatched to the scientific and experimental base within the Moscow Military District (MVO) for conversion to two-seat configuration (UTI).

It has also been uncovered that a UTI aircraft underwent trials during October 1945 at NII VVS (Scientific Research Institute of the Air Force) located at Zhukovsky Airfield to the south-east of Moscow (now Zhukovsky International Airport). This may potentially have been Spitfire Mk.IX MJ800 but is not confirmed.

Further conversions were undertaken, potentially as many as fifty (50). It is understood that one, and possibly more, of these conversions were carried out in Leningrad (now St. Petersburg) at No.1 ARB (*Aviatsionnaya Remontnaya Baza*/ Aircraft Repair Base).

It has also been confirmed that UTIs were flown by 26, and potentially 27, GIAP (Guards Fighter Aviation Regiment) which were based in the Leningrad area.

Front view of the UTI shown at the top of the page. Note Ilyushin Il-2 aircraft behind. *(Image: via Wojtek Matusiak collection)*

The above image, albeit of poor quality, shows a Soviet Air Force UTI at NII VVS (Scientific Research Institute of the Air Force) located at Zhukovsky Airfield. There is the potential that this is Spitfire Mk.IX MJ800, as she was converted in this area. Note the distinctive hexagonal-patterned apron, along with star under the wing and on the spinner. *(Image: via Wojtek Matusiak collection)*

Although details of the UTI aircraft are sparse, there are several unsubstantiated stories related to them. These stories include UTI production being carried out in Tbilisi, Georgia, or that the rear cockpit was equipped with flying controls which does seem unlikely, or even that some of the Soviet UTI aircraft may have been passed to the Chinese Air Force who had requested Spitfire Mk.IX's from the Soviet Union.

In the absence of any supporting evidence, it is not possible to confirm any of these stories. It is believed that all Soviet Air Force UTI converted aircraft were broken up and scrapped.

Lt. V.M. Mukhmediarov (3rd from left), pilot of 14 GIAP being shown around a Spitfire UTI. Note twin cockpit canopies, and wing cannons blanked-off. *(Image: Oleg Korytov/www.airforce.ru)*

In the Leningrad area during the summer of 1945, Lt. Col. V.A. Matsiyevich C/O 26 GIAP (Guards Fighter Aviation Regiment) reads instructions to pilots and mechanics of his regiment in front of a Spitfire UTI. Note the generous gap around the rear cockpit canopy. *(Image: Peter Arnold Collection)*

Final instructions from Lt. Col. Matsiyevich (centre) before take-off. Note same pilots as image at top of page, and potentially the same aircraft. Also take note of pointed rudder with white lower section. *(Image: via Wojtek Matusiak collection)*

ES127

Spitfire ES127 is the only known Mk.V airframe converted to two-seat configuration.

Built at the Castle Bromwich factory as a Mk.V with a Vokes Tropical filter beneath the Rolls Royce Merlin 46 engine, ES127 was accepted by the RAF and delivered to 39 MU at Colerne, Wiltshire on 10 November 1942. She passed to 82 MU at RAF Lichfield in Staffordshire a few weeks later, on 27 November 1942, in preparation for her shipment to the Mediterranean theatre of operations.

Dispatched, possibly from Birkenhead docks, on 11 December 1942 aboard the *SS Empire Clive* bound for Takoradi in Ghana, ES127 arrived on 23 January 1943.

There are no known mentions of squadron service for ES127 prior to 6 April 1943, when she appears in the 417 (City of Windsor) Sqn. RCAF Operational Record Book (ORB). It was on this day that ES127 was flown by F/O R.L. Patterson on a Convoy protection mission, which was the first of eighteen missions recorded with the squadron.

Her final mission with 417 Sqn. was on 28 April 1943 when she was flown by F/L W.H Pentland on a sweep over the battle area.

ES127 is recorded as moving to North Africa on 30 November 1943, but there are no details of the squadron with which she was serving. However, it is known she served with 4 Sqn. SAAF around this time, with whom she wore the codes *KJ-I* along with a red tip on the rudder.

ES127 passed to a Maintenance Unit at Catania-Fontannrossa Airfield, Sicily in the latter part of 1943. It was at this time that she was locally adapted to accommodate a second seat in place of the fuel tanks directly in front of the pilot.

The image of ES127 at Catania Airfield, Sicily during early 1944 clearly shows the second windscreen. Worthy of note is the lack of a sliding hood fitted to the front cockpit, this would therefore make for a very breezy and somewhat uncomfortable ride!

This rare image of ES127 shows her at Catania Airfield, Sicily in early 1944, following the addition of the second cockpit. Note Mount Etna in the background. *(Image: Peter Arnold Collection)*

With the removal of the main fuselage fuel tanks to accommodate the second seat, it can be safely assumed that fuel tanks were installed in the wings. The additional seat would have been very cramped and therefore flying controls would not be fitted.

Following conversion ES127 was allocated to 261 Sqn. RAF. She would have been used as a Squadron *hack* or in a communications role and not for front-line fighter duties. ES127 was struck off RAF charge on 8 March 1944 and allocated to ground instructional status. It is believed that ES127 was eventually broken up and scrapped.

An interesting footnote to this story is that during the restoration of single-seat Spitfire Mk.IX RR232, which coincidently is also an ex. SAAF aircraft, a similar *jump-seat* configuration was mocked-up. This image taken on 14 September 2004 shows the small dimensions of the space to good effect. *(Image: Peter Arnold)*

A PRIVATE VENTURE

A two-seat trainer version of the Spitfire was first suggested by Vickers-Armstrongs Ltd as early as 1941, but as production would detract from much-needed operational types there was no appetite from the Air Ministry and the idea was dropped.

However, the idea was revived as a private venture by Vickers when they purchased Spitfire Mk.VIII MT818 back from the Air Ministry in February 1945 and converted her to Type 502 specification to become the Spitfire High-Speed Trainer Prototype *(see MT818)*.

The prototype flew on 9 September 1946 initially with Class B marks *N-32* then later with civilian registration G-AIDN. She underwent a thorough testing and trials programme.

A second Spitfire Mk.VIII Trainer aircraft was planned but did not proceed. G-AKBD was earmarked for conversion to two-seat specification. Whilst the RAF serial of the airframe is unknown, the manufacturer allocated construction number 6S/730847 for the converted aircraft. There are mentions of G-AKBD being completed in the latter half of 1947, however there is no known documentation to confirm that this conversion was carried out. The civilian registration was struck off the register on 31 May 1948.

It was now February 1948, but there was still no interest from the Air Ministry in the Spitfire Trainer design. The reasons given for the lack of interest were that the Spitfire was 'virtually extinct' in RAF service, the RAF were already committed to basic trainer types which had been designed to meet their specific requirements, and that the Auxiliary Fighter Squadrons which were mooted as a possible recipient of the type already had plans to convert to jet types. A career in the RAF for the Spitfire Trainer was looking highly unlikely.

There was however a glimmer of hope in March 1949, when Fighter Command expressed an interest in the Spitfire Trainer design for a requirement within the Auxiliary Squadrons. In addition, the Royal Navy toyed with the idea of replacing their Harvard intermediate trainer aircraft with Spitfire Trainers.

A demonstration of the prototype G-AIDN to RAF Reserve Command took place at White Waltham on 11 April 1949 with a favourable outcome of a possible requirement for approximately twenty (20) aircraft. The requirement was to bridge the gap between the Harvard and the Spitfire Mk.22 within the Auxiliary Squadrons.

Unfortunately, this possible requirement did not equate to an order. Whilst this was the end of the story for the Spitfire Trainer and a potential role in the RAF, there were already expressions of interest from further afield and these are detailed later in the book.

MT818 at rest, Biggin Hill, 24 May 2016. *(Image: Greg Davis)*

Prototype MT818

MT818 is a significant aircraft; she is the only surviving Spitfire prototype across the entire vast range of marks and types. She was originally built as a single-seat Mk. VIII at the Vickers-Armstrongs factory, Eastleigh, emerging in June 1944. She was allocated to the Controller of Research and Development, High Post Airfield by mid-June 1944 and used in comparison trials before being transferred back to Vickers-Armstrongs Ltd. in February 1945.

Vickers converted MT818 into the prototype Type 502 Mk. VIII Trainer (conversion construction number 6S/729058), and she undertook her first flight in this configuration on 9 September 1946 at Chilbolton. In order to accommodate the second cockpit within the airframe the front cockpit was moved forward by 13½ inches thus reducing the main fuel tanks capacity (down from 96 to 39 gallons), and this was supplemented by placing additional tanks in the wings.

MT818 as a single-seat aircraft prior to conversion to the prototype Spitfire Trainer. She is seen here at High Post Airfield in Wiltshire during 1944. *(Image: Charles E Brown via Peter Arnold collection)*

MT818 wearing an all-over yellow colour scheme and civilian registration G-AIDN at RAF Odiham, 1947. *(Image: Peter Arnold Collection)*

Each wing contained two fuel tanks, one in the wing leading edge of 12¾ gallons, with another of 14¼ gallons behind the spar in the gun bay. Fitted with a Rolls-Royce Merlin 66 (No.179907), MT818 retained four 0.303 Browning machine guns (two per wing, in the two outer wing bays) for weapons training.

Flight testing was carried out by Vickers test pilot Mike Lithgow. It was observed during these tests that MT818 tightened in the turn, and to counter this behaviour a 9½lb "bob" weight was fitted into the elevator circuit. In addition, a 7¾ inch long piece of 'L' shaped metal was added to the elevator trailing edge on both the upper and lower surfaces. These are retained to this day *(see MT818 Miscellany)*. The elevator additions were not however incorporated into the later Mk.IX Trainer aircraft.

MT818 at Radlett for the SBAC display in 1947. Note larger style civilian registration. *(Image: Peter Arnold collection)*

Above: MT818/G-AIDN at the inaugural SBAC (Society of British Aircraft Constructors) flying display and exhibition held at Farnborough Airfield, during 1948. *(Image: Peter Arnold collection)*

Right: MT818/G-AIDN participating in the Elmdon National Air Races on 1 August 1949, wearing a very smart silver and dark blue scheme. *(Image: Peter Arnold Collection)*

MT818 taking part in the Kings Cup race, 1950. *(Image: Peter Arnold Collection)*

Initially MT818 carried the Class-B marks *N32* during testing, but later wore the civilian registration G-AIDN.

In February 1947, G-AIDN was dispatched to the Aeroplane and Armament Experimental Establishment (A&AEE) at RAF Boscombe Down for handling trials, however whilst the RAF report found her performance like a single-seat Spitfire aircraft, it also highlighted the poor visibility from the rear cockpit. No orders were placed by the RAF *(see Appendix for full report)*. MT818 unfortunately suffered a wheels-up landing on 18 September 1948.

MT818 participated in numerous demonstrations and air-races until 1953 when she was returned to Chilbolton and placed in storage.

Billy Butlin posing with MT818 at Biggin Hill in July 1959, prior to the London-Paris Air Race. *(Image: Peter Arnold collection)*

MT818 at Staverton, 23 April 1967. *(Image: Peter Foote via Peter Arnold Collection)*

Following disposal by Vickers, MT818 was released to Vivian Bellamy, who flew it to the Hampshire Aeroplane Club at Eastleigh on 31 August 1956. MT818 won the piston-engine category after taking part in the *Daily Mail* London-Paris Air Race during 1959, with pilot Viv Bellamy and Billy Butlin (famous holiday camp owner) in the back seat.

Acquired by John Fairey and Anthony Stone on August 1963, MT818 remained at Eastleigh initially before moving to Andover where she was maintained in an

airworthy condition. It was around this time that she received an all-over pale blue colour scheme.

The ownership of MT818 changed in January 1968, when Tim Davies bought a half-share in the aircraft. Around this time, MT818 adopted a royal-blue scheme with white cheatlines, but this was replaced in the 1970s with an all-over yellow scheme once more with the registration G-AIDN on the rear fuselage.

MT818 on the grass at Andover, 31 July 1969. *(Image: Ron Cranham via Peter Arnold Collection)*

This shot, taken on the same day as the image at the bottom of the previous page, 31 July 1969, shows an incredibly pleased Spitfire Historian!! Peter Arnold seen here after flying in G-AIDN. Half a century later and fellow co-author Greg Davis would fly in the same aircraft. *(Image: Ron Cranham via Peter Arnold Collection)*

In 1976, MT818 was acquired by Maurice Bayliss and registered as G-AIDN on 29 September that year. However, ownership was short when on 20 November 1976 MT818 was registered to Tarrant W.R. Case and based at Baginton, Warwickshire.

Less than a year later, on 22 September 1977, ownership changed again when MT818 was registered to Graham F. Miller of Cardiff, Wales. MT818 suffered damage, on 6 February 1977, due to undercarriage issues on landing at Baginton.

MT818 at the Battle of Britain display, RAF St. Athan in September 1982. *(Image: John Sanderson collection)*

MT818 at Medford, Oregon, USA, circa 1988. *(Image: Peter Arnold Collection)*

Repair work commenced at Baginton until 1980 when MT818 was transported to RAF St Athan for the work to continue. She was assembled, albeit not fully repaired, and displayed at the Battle of Britain display held at the base in September 1982 wearing a new glossy camouflage scheme with the codes *G-M* to reflect her owner's initials.

MT818 was transported to Houston, Texas following her owner upon his move to the USA. She was reassembled by early 1985 at Williams Airport and underwent engine runs in July of the same year. She was acquired by Jack Ericson of Oregon in early 1986 and registered as N58JE. MT818 was flown to her owner's museum located at Tillamook, Oregon in 1993 where she was placed on static display.

MT818 in the *Personal Plane Services* workshop, Wycombe Air Park on 10 January 2011. *(Image: Richard Paver)*

MT818 on display at the Chelsea Masterpiece show in London on 4 July 2011. *(Image: Peter Arnold)*

Purchased by Provenance Fighter Sales in April 2007 and registered N818MT, MT818 was transported by road to French Valley Airport, Murrieta, California the following month. MT818 had never undergone restoration and was therefore offered for sale in original 'as-is' condition.

Subsequently acquired by Paul Andrews on 18 May 2007, MT818 was transported to the UK, arriving on 25 September 2007. After a short period at the owner's property in West Sussex she was moved to Kemble Airfield for a thorough inspection of the airframe.

MT818 was re-registered as G-AIDN on 4 March 2008 and transported to *Personal Plane Services* at Wycombe Air Park (Booker) in August 2010, who were commissioned to carefully refurbish MT818 back to airworthy condition. Work complete in March 2016, MT818 was transferred to the *Biggin Hill Heritage Hangar* and is now operated by *Warbird Experiences Ltd* for customer experience flights when required.

MT818 upon arrival at Biggin Hill, 31 March 2016. Note colour of spinner and fuselage band. *(Image: John Sanderson)*

Co-author Greg Davis pointing out the fuel tank positions in the wing of MT818 during a two-seat Spitfire focussed event at the *Biggin Hill Heritage Hangar*. November 2019. *(Image: Peter Green)*

Prototype Spitfire Trainer Mk.VIII MT818 with Mk.IX MJ627 beyond, Biggin Hill, 2016. Note smaller door for access to rear cockpit. *(Image: Greg Davis)*

Above: Note the small angled metal additions to the elevator either side of the trim tab. This is unique to MT818 and not replicated on production aircraft. *(Image: Fred Mussard)*

Above: MT818 is uniquely equipped with an anti-spin parachute located in a hatch in the rear fuselage. Only installed on the prototype and not on production aircraft. *(Image: Fred Mussard)*

Left: Built as a Mk.VIII, MT818 is the only Spitfire Trainer to have a retractable tailwheel. Note the closed tail wheel doors with the previous all-over yellow colour scheme showing through. These doors would not normally close with the tailwheel down but have been modified to allow it to be locked in the down position. *(Image: Fred Mussard)*

Two-seat Spitfire Prototype Mk.VIII MT818 along with Mk.IX MJ627 flying over Biggin Hill during 2016. (Image: Richard Paver)

MARKETING THE SPITFIRE TRAINER

Following the successful conversion and testing of Mk.VIII MT818, Vickers-Armstrongs Ltd set about "marketing" the concept of the Spitfire High Speed Trainer. It is worth noting that the two-seat version of the Spitfire was referred to in a capitalised form within all official Vickers documentation (i.e. Spitfire TRAINER) and not as a Tr.8 or Tr.9 which is a modern-day designation not used by the manufacturer. MT818 was demonstrated widely by Vickers to market the design.

See Appendix for sales brochure produced by Vickers-Armstrongs Ltd to support their marketing and sales efforts for the Spitfire High Speed Trainer.

Right: The original Vickers Spitfire TRAINER sales model. Handmade in wood, she lives in her original case. The model is in the custodianship of co-author Peter Arnold.

Left: Vickers-Armstrongs Ltd advertisement for the Spitfire High Speed Trainer as featured in Flight Magazine during 1946.

Right: Feature in French aviation magazine *Decollage*, 1947.

Superb colour image of MT818 wearing overall yellow colour scheme and Class B marks N32, following her conversion to two-seat Trainer configuration, circa 1946. *(Image: Charles E Brown / Vickers / Peter Arnold collection)*

ORDER BOOK ACTIVITY

Following extensive marketing and demonstrations using the prototype Spitfire Trainer, Mk.VIII MT818/G-AIDN, Vickers-Armstrongs Ltd. received several orders and enquiries from various Air Arms around the world.

It was decided by Vickers to utilise surplus Spitfire Mk.IX airframes as the basis for production and a quantity of ex-RAF machines were re-purchased from the Air Ministry for the purpose of conversion to two-seat Trainer configuration.

It is worthy of note, that all Spitfire Trainer aircraft were originally built as single-seat aircraft and subsequently converted by Vickers following purchase from the Air Ministry in the post-war period.

There were a number of minor differences between the Prototype Mk.VIII and Production Mk.IX aircraft, these included the removal of the anti-spin parachute in the rear fuselage, an overall reduction in fuel capacity from 93 to 90 gallons (see Note A below), and the obvious difference of the Prototype being equipped with the retractable tailwheel of the Mk.VIII, whereas the Mk.IX had the fixed tailwheel of that Spitfire mark.

A series of sales demonstration tours were undertaken by Vickers to try to increase sales for the Spitfire Trainer including one in June 1947 when the prototype MT818/G-AIDN was flown across to Belgium, but there was no interest and no new orders were forthcoming.

A further sales tour was undertaken in October 1949, when Vickers chief test pilot Jeffrey Quill along with P.G. Roberts flew Mk.IX Trainer G-ALJM (See Egypt ML113) to Scandinavia. Arriving in Copenhagen, Denmark on 12 October, and then on to Gothenburg, Sweden, eventually arriving in Oslo, Norway on 18 October.

Norway did express interest in converting some of their existing single-seat Mk.IX aircraft to two-seat configuration and were quoted a price of between £5,200 and £5,700 each. No agreement was reached, and no orders were placed.

Note A – Differences in fuel capacity between the Prototype Mk.VIII and Production Mk.IX aircraft

- Prototype Mk.VIII: Main tank: 39 gallons, Each wing: 1 off 14¼ gallon & 1 off 12¾ gallon tanks
- Production Mk.IX: Main tank: 38 gallons, Each wing: 1 off 13½ gallon & 1 off 12½ gallon tanks

Orders Received

Country	Delivered by	Order Size	Notes
Netherlands	23 March 1948	3 Aircraft	
India	15 November 1948	10 Aircraft	
Egypt	13 April 1950	1 Aircraft	Potential additional aircraft, not confirmed
Ireland	30 July 1951	6 Aircraft	
Argentina	-	10 Aircraft	Order placed in the 1950s, later cancelled
Iraq	-	6 Aircraft	Order placed in the 1950s, later cancelled

A total of thirty-six (36) Spitfire Trainer aircraft ordered, with twenty (20) delivered.

Spitfire Trainer Development

Vickers-Armstrongs Ltd undertook to further develop the two-seat Trainer concept, but with diminishing sales interest all efforts were subsequently wound down.

However, and before all efforts were halted, other Spitfire marks were assessed to determine their suitability for conversion to two-seat Trainer configuration and they are outlined below.

Spitfire Mk.XVI

The Spitfire Mk.XVI was considered for conversion. The airframe is essentially a Mk.IX fitted with a US Packard Motor Car Company licence-built Merlin engine. The engineering required to convert this mark to two-seat configuration would therefore utilise the established development for the Mk.IX Trainer which was already in production. There were other minor modifications away from the Mk.IX Trainer design, the alternative engine has been mentioned, but also included an increase in fuel capacity from 90 to 94 gallons.

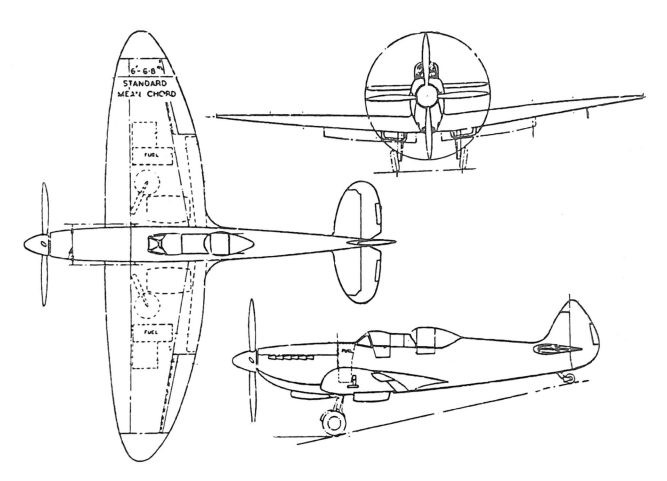

Mk.XVI Trainer general arrangement. *(Image: Vickers)*

Spitfire Mk.XVIII

The Mk.XVIII, a later low-back Griffon-engine powered mark, was also considered for conversion to two-seat configuration. It is known that Vickers-Armstrongs began development under Type number 518 and some drawings were produced, but unfortunately no surviving copies are known to exist.

FULFILLED ORDERS

This chapter details the various Air Arms around the world who operated the Spitfire Trainer aircraft along with the individual aircraft histories.

Below is a breakdown of the deliveries of all known Vickers-Armstrongs Ltd. converted Spitfire Trainer aircraft.

Country	Aircraft serial		Delivery date
Netherlands	BS147	(H-99)	23 March 1948
	BS274	(H-98)	23 March 1948
	MK715	(H-97)	23 March 1948
India	MA848	(HS534)	3 June 1948
	MH432	(HS535)	September 1948
	MJ177	(HS536)	29 September 1948
	MJ276	(HS537)	29 September 1948
	MJ451	(HS538)	September 1948
	MJ518	(HS539)	November 1948
	MK172	(HS540)	15 November 1948
	MK176	(HS541)	15 November 1948
	MK298	(HS542)	15 November 1948
	ML417	(HS543)	15 November 1948
Egypt *	ML113	(684)	13 April 1950
Ireland	MJ627	(158)	5 June 1951
	MJ772	(159)	5 June 1951
	MK721	(160)	29 June 1951
	PV202	(161)	29 June 1951
	ML407	(162)	30 July 1951
	TE308	(163)	30 July 1951

* Unconfirmed reports of one (1), possibly two (2), additional aircraft provided to Egypt. See investigative piece in the Appendix entitled 'An Egyptian Mystery' for further details.

The following pages are arranged from the first Spitfire Trainer operator through to the last.

THE NETHERLANDS

The Royal Netherlands Air Force (RNethAF) purchased 77 Spitfires following World War II, including three Mk.IX Trainer aircraft. The aircraft were converted at Eastleigh by Vickers-Armstrongs Ltd. and delivered to the Netherlands on 23 March 1948.

RAF Serial	Class B Marks	RNethAF Serial
BS147	G.15-1	H-99, 3W-22
BS274	N-42	H-98, 3W-20
MK715	N-41	H-97, 3W-21

The three aircraft at Eastleigh before delivery to the RNethAF. *(Image: Vickers)*

Posed photograph to commemorate the handover of the three Spitfire Trainer aircraft to the Royal Netherlands Air Force. Taken on 23 March 1948 at Eastleigh prior to departure. *(Image: Peter Arnold collection)*

BS147 (H-99)

Built at Eastleigh as a single-seat Spitfire Mk.IX, BS147 flew for the first time on 20 August 1942. She served with 401 (City of Westmount) Sqn. RCAF, based at RAF Kenley from 1 September 1942.

Whilst with 401 Sqn., BS147 carried out Channel fighter sweeps along with bomber escorting missions. She was flown by several different pilots from the squadron and kept highly active. On 16 October 1942, when returning from a bomber escort sortie with Flt. Lt. D.C. Morrison DFM at the controls, BS147 was damaged when she was caught in the slipstream of the preceding aircraft and lost height more quickly than expected. BS147 undershot the runway, managed to go around again and subsequently crashed at Biggin Hill suffering Cat.Ac damage, meaning the repairs were beyond the unit's capability. BS147 was subsequently repaired.

The next known mention of BS147 within the official RAF records is in March 1945 when she is serving with 310 (Czech) Sqn. then based at RAF Manston in Kent, with the allocated codes *NN-E*.

Sold to Vickers-Armstrongs Ltd., converted to Spitfire Trainer configuration, and sold to the Royal Netherlands Air Force (RNethAF) as a two-seat advanced trainer.

Sent back to Eastleigh for conversion by Vickers-Armstrongs Ltd. to two-seat Trainer configuration, BS147 was tested and accepted by the RNethAF on 22 March 1948. Flown to the Fighter Pilot Training School (JVS), Twenthe Air Force Base, Netherlands the following day and was allocated the RNethAF serial *H-99*. She was used to train pilots before they went solo on the single-seat version of the Spitfire Mk.IX aircraft.

BS147 was allocated to 322 Sqn. RNethAF in early 1950, for use by reserve pilots and marked as *3W-22*. She suffered a belly landing on 13 May 1953, but was quickly repaired, and continued serving with 322 Sqn. until September 1953 when she was placed in open storage.

Having been struck off charge, she was sold to Schreiner Aero Contractors and flown to their base at Ypenburg Airport, Netherlands, on 22 September 1954.

Flt. Sgt. Vojtech Skreka-Badouin (right) and his mechanic standing in front of BS147 at Manston during June 1945. *(Image: Zdenek Hurt via Peter Arnold collection)*

Above: Superb image of BS147 in RNethAF colours as *H-99*, circa 1948. Note later style *'99'* codes. *(Image: Herman Dekker)*

Above: BS147 (H-99) in later all-over silver colour scheme. *(Image: Peter Arnold collection)*

BS147 (H-99) at Soesterberg during 1952, when serving with 322 Sqn. as 3W-22. *(Image: Harry Van Der Meer collection)*

It was at this time that BS147 was registered as PH-NFN and modified for target-towing duties. She received an overall orange colour scheme and sported *Donald Duck* nose-art on her engine cowlings. On 22 November 1955 during a test flight, Pilot Ben de Geus overshot the landing which resulted in damage to one wing. The wing was replaced and BS147 resumed target-towing duties for the Royal Netherlands Army.

BS147 (PH-NFN) when with Schreiner Aero at Ypenburg Airport for target-towing duties. *(Image: Peter Arnold collection)*

BS147 suffered another landing accident on 4 May 1957 at Texel Airfield. Pilot Ben de Geus deployed the undercarriage selector to the *Down* position, but his passenger managed to get their fingers caught within the same mechanism in the rear cockpit without the pilot's knowledge. Unfortunately, this meant that the undercarriage was not fully locked down and upon landing it collapsed, with BS147 sliding to a stop on her belly. BS147 was not repaired, and she was duly broken up on site at Texel with her remains observed within a scrapyard in Haarlem, Netherlands during 1958.

BS147 (PH-NFN) following her landing accident at Texel, Netherlands on 4 May 1957. Note rear cockpit glazing split in two and subsequently repaired with metal 'staples' as a makeshift repair to hold the pieces together. *(Image: Herman Dekker)*

Another view of BS147 (PH-NFN) on her belly at Texel Airfield on 4 May 1957, clearly showing the target drogue wrapped around the starboard wing. *(Image: Herman Dekker)*

BS147 in the snow at Ypenburg Airport. Note lack of civilian registration on fuselage. *(Image: Harry Van Der Meer)*

This rear cockpit shot from BS147 shows her civilian identity to good effect. Beyond are two of the other Spitfires operated by Schreiner Aero, albeit single-seat variants. *(Image: Harry Van Der Meer)*

BS147 (PH-NFN) at Ypenburg Airport, Netherlands in 1956. At this time, she was operated by Schreiner Aero Contractors towing target drogues and wears a high visibility colour scheme of all-over orange. Note Donald Duck nose art on engine cowling. *(Image: Peter Arnold collection)*

BS274 (H-98)

BS274 was built at Rolls Royce Hucknall as a Mk.IX, converted from a Mk.V, and flown for the first time on 12 August 1942. She was incorrectly painted with the spurious serial *BF274* which was subsequently worn throughout her career.

BS274 did not serve with a front-line squadron, but she was however, allocated to the Aeroplane & Armament Experimental Establishment (A&AEE) at Boscombe Down in December 1942 for performance and fuel consumption trials. Having been passed to the Flight Refuelling Company at RAF Ford, Sussex for fighter towing trials in July 1944, she was subsequently sold back

to Vickers-Armstrongs Ltd. at Eastleigh on 11 January 1947 for conversion to Type 509 two-seat specification. BS274 was subsequently sold to the Royal Netherlands Air Force (RNethAF).

Like the other Spitfire Mk.IX Trainers sold to the Netherlands, BS274 was tested by the RNethAF on 17 March 1948 before delivery on 23 March 1948. She formed part of the Fighter Pilot Training School (JVS) at Twenthe Air Force Base in the Netherlands, where she was allocated the serial *H-98*.

Two images of BS274 (*'BF274'*) prior to her conversion to two-seat Spitfire Trainer configuration. *(Images: Vickers)*

BS274 (H-98) with her sister-ships behind on 23 March 1948 prior to delivery to the Netherlands. *(Image: Vickers)*

BS274 suffered a minor belly landing at Twenthe Air Force Base on 16 May 1949 but was quickly repaired. She was flown by Prince Bernhard (Consort to Queen Juliana of the Netherlands) for his final Spitfire sortie on 14 August 1950. She was then assigned to 322 Sqn. RNethAF and allocated the codes *3W-20*, which were never applied, and she retained the earlier marks *H-98*.

On 7 February 1951 BS274 suffered a collapsed undercarriage on landing was declared beyond economical repair (Cat.E) and subsequently scrapped.

BS274 in RNethAF service as *H-98*. Note later style *'98'* code. *(Image: Peter Arnold collection)*

MK715 (H-97)

Built as a single-seat Mk.IX, MK715 was allocated to 56 Sqn. at RAF Newchurch, Kent on 9 May 1944. She was subsequently passed to 402 (City of Winnipeg) Sqn. RCAF on 17 July 1944, and then 1 Sqn. on 12 April 1945 where she flew missions over Northern Europe.

Sold back to her original manufacturers, Vickers-Armstrongs Ltd. at Eastleigh, on 2 January 1947 for conversion to Type 509 two-seat specification, MK715 was then sold to the Royal Netherlands Air Force (RNethAF).

MK715 was tested by RNethAF test-pilot Vijzelaar on 9 March 1948 and flown, along with BS147 & BS274, to the Netherlands on 23 March 1948. She was allotted to the Fighter Pilot Training School (JVS) at Twenthe Air Force Base and allocated the RNethAF serial H-97.

MK715 was used to convert pilots from the North American Harvard advanced trainer to the single-seat Spitfire Mk.IX, as well as communications flight duties.

Whilst with the JVS, MK715 suffered a minor belly-landing at Twenthe on 1 June 1950 due to her undercarriage not locking down, but she was back flying again by 20 June. MK715 was allocated to 322 Sqn. RNethAF in February 1951 and given the codes 3W-21. She relocated with the squadron when they moved to Soesterberg on 31 August 1951.

Unfortunately, she suffered a fatal accident on 20 September 1951 sadly killing Lt. A. van Tienhoven and injuring Capt. J.D. Sandberg. MK715 was struck off charge and scrapped at Soesterberg in October 1951.

Right: MK715 in RNethAF service. Note RAF serial on tail. *(Image: Peter Arnold collection)*

MK715 at Eastleigh Aerodrome before delivery to the Netherlands, March 1948. *(Image: Vickers)*

INDIA

The Royal Indian Air Force (RIAF) purchased over one hundred and fifty (150) Spitfires of varying marks, including ten (10) Mk.IX Trainer aircraft. All RIAF Spitfire Trainers were delivered to India by 15 November 1948.

RAF Serial	*Class B Marks*	*RIAF Serial*
MA848	*G.15-2*	*HS534*
MH432	*G,15-3*	*HS535*
MJ177	*G.15-4*	*HS536*
MJ276	*G.15-5*	*HS537*
MJ451	*G.15-6*	*HS538*
MJ518	*G.15-7*	*HS539*
MK172	*G.15-8*	*HS540*
MK176	*G.15-9*	*HS541*
MK298	*G.15-10*	*HS542*
ML417	*G.15-11*	*HS543*

The RIAF believed that as part of their second order for Mk.XVIII aircraft, the final four (4) aircraft of that order would be provided as two-seat Trainers. This has not been confirmed, and none were built or delivered in this configuration.

Vickers-Armstrongs Ltd. did however produce some drawings for the Mk.XVIII Trainer under Type number 518, but no further development work was carried out.

Of the ten Spitfire Trainers supplied to the RIAF only one intact aircraft is known to remain today, ML417/HS543, albeit in single-seat configuration. The other nine aircraft were apparently broken up; however, the substantial remains of MJ518/HS539 are retained in storage in India.

Three RIAF Spitfire Mk.IX Trainers at Ambala Air Force Base, India during 1948. Note aircraft all wear individual number identifiers and are, from left to right, No.81/HS535 (RAF serial MH432), No.82* and No.80*. (* RIAF and RAF serials unknown). *(Image: Peter Arnold collection)*

MA848 (HS534)

Built at the Castle Bromwich shadow factory near Birmingham, MA848 was delivered to 6 MU at RAF Brize Norton on 27 June 1943. Allocated to 129 Sqn., Hornchurch, Essex on 4 August 1943 with codes *DV-T*, MA848 became the mount of P/O Bradshaw.

The squadron Operational Record Book (ORB) shows MA848 taking part in five Ramrod missions escorting bombers to northern Europe. Her time with the squadron was short-lived however, as by 27 August she was at Heston with 405 Aircraft Repair Flight.

Having been reallocated to 131 (County of Kent) Sqn., at Redhill on 27 September 1943, with codes *NX-U*, MA848 went through several short-term postings going to 165 (Ceylon) Sqn. at Culmhead, Somerset on 19 March 1944, before 453 (RAAF) Sqn. on 11 April at Ford, West Sussex, and then to 33 Sqn. at North Weald, Essex on 16 May.

There was another move on 23 May 1944, with MA848 going to Northolt and the Station Flight until 8 July when she joined 310 (Czech) Sqn. at Lympne, Kent. The final operational posting for MA848 was on 15 July 1944 to 504 (County of Nottingham) Sqn. at Detling, Kent.

Her front-line career now over, MA848 arrived at 58 OTU, RAF Grangemouth, near Fife, Scotland on 5 April 1945 to train new pilots.

Sold back to Vickers-Armstrongs Ltd. on 22 January 1947 and subsequently converted to Type 509 Spitfire Trainer configuration, MA848 became part of the order for the Royal Indian Air Force (RIAF). She flew for the first time as a two-seat aircraft wearing the Class-B marks *G.15-2* before delivery to the RIAF on 3 June 1948. She was allocated serial HS534 in RIAF service.

In RIAF service MA848 was allocated to No.2 Flying Training School (FTS) at Jodhpur, India, in 1948, before transferring to the Advanced Flying School (AFS) at Ambala Air Force Base in 1949 to train pilots converting to Spitfire Mk.XVIII and Tempest II aircraft. This duty was taken over by Spitfire Mk.XVIII aircraft during 1952, and all Spitfire Mk.IX Trainers were retired by the end of 1953.

The fate of MA848 is unknown, but it is believed she was broken up.

HS534 (RAF serial MA848) was the first Spitfire Trainer to be supplied to the RIAF, seen here wearing the short-lived, and inaccurate, *Chakra* markings at the Vickers factory prior to dispatch, 1948. These markings were an incorrect interpretation by Vickers and quickly replaced with an RIAF roundel upon arrival in India. *(Image: Wojtek Matusiak collection)*

HS534 (RAF serial MA848) in later markings, Ambala, 1948. *(Image: Peter Arnold collection)*

MH432 (HS535)

MH432 was built at the Castle Bromwich factory near Birmingham. Accepted by the RAF, she was allocated to 222 (Natal) Sqn. at Hornchurch, Essex on 13 August 1943. She passed to 84 Group Support Unit (GSU) of the 2nd Tactical Air Force (TAF) on 20 May 1944 and was assigned to 442 (Caribou) Sqn. RCAF, based at RAF Digby, Lincolnshire on 11 January 1945.

There was a further reassignment for MH432 on 21 March 1945 when she moved to 401 (City of Westmount) Sqn. RCAF becoming the mount of F/L W.R. Tew. A final operational posting for MH432 within the RAF came on 17 May 1945 when she was allocated to 130 (Punjab) Sqn. which was in the process of repatriating back to RAF North Weald, Essex.

Sold back to Vickers-Armstrongs on 17 October 1946, MH432 underwent conversion to Type 509 Spitfire Trainer configuration for the Royal Indian Air Force (RIAF). She flew for the first time as a two-seat aircraft on 15 May 1948 wearing the Class-B marks *G.15-3* before delivery to the RIAF on 29 September 1948.

In RIAF service, MH432 was allocated the serial HS535 and assigned to the Advanced Flying School (AFS) at Ambala Air Force Base, India, in 1949 where she provided dual instruction capability for pilots converting to the more powerful Spitfire Mk.XVIII and Tempest II aircraft.

MH432 is believed to have been broken up.

HS535 (RAF serial MH432) on the ramp at Ambala Air Force Base, India, during 1948. *(Image: Peter Arnold collection)*

MJ177 (HS536)

Built as an LF Mk.IX at the Castle Bromwich factory, MJ177 was taken on charge by the RAF at 39 MU, Colerne on 16 October 1943. Assigned to 340 (Île-de-France) Sqn. at Perranporth in Cornwall on 23 January 1944, MJ177 was allocated the codes *GW-S*. She joined the squadron around the same time as MJ518 *(see MJ518)* which was also later converted to two-seat configuration for the RIAF. Due to bad weather in the area, the first operational flight with the squadron was not until 13 February when S/Lt. I. Porchon, piloting MJ177, led Blue section on a Convoy Patrol to the south-west of Plymouth, without incident. She was re-assigned to 421 (Red Indian) Sqn. RCAF at Tangmere, West Sussex on 8 June 1944 before moving on to the Test Flight of 34 Wing on 28 September of the same year.

Purchased back by Vickers-Armstrongs on 16 April 1947, MJ177 was converted to two-seat Spitfire Trainer configuration as part of the order for the Royal Indian Air Force (RIAF). MJ177 flew for the first time as a two-seat aircraft on 11 May 1948 wearing the Class-B marks *G.15-4* before being delivered to the RIAF in September 1948.

Allocated the RIAF serial HS536, MJ177 was assigned to the Advanced Flying School (AFS) at Ambala Air Force Base, India, in 1949. All Spitfire Trainer aircraft in RIAF service were struck off charge in 1953, and it is understood MJ177 was broken up.

MJ276 (HS537)

Emerging from the Castle Bromwich shadow factory as an LF Mk.IX aircraft, MJ276 was taken on charge by the RAF and arrived at 39 MU, Colerne on 3 November

1943. A little over a week later, on 12 November, MJ276 was dispatched to 405 Aircraft Repair Flight (ARF) at

Heston before being allocated to 602 (City of Glasgow) Squadron.

MJ276 was flown by New Zealander F/O M.D. Morgan on 6 June 1944 (D-Day) providing cover for the ground forces over the beaches of Normandy, France. Whilst she was recorded as Missing/FTR (failed to return) on the 15 June 1944 and struck off charge, MJ276 was subsequently brought back on charge and spent time with 405 Repair & Salvage Unit (RSU) at Detling, Kent before allocation to 453 (RAAF) Sqn. in August 1944. A final RAF operational assignment was made on 14 September 1944 when MJ276 went to 441 (Silver Fox) Sqn. RCAF before she was allocated to 82 Group Communication Flight on 19 July 1945.

Sold to Vickers-Armstrongs on 16 April 1947, MJ276 was converted to Type 509 at Eastleigh for the Royal Indian Air Force (RIAF). Taking to the skies for a first flight as a two-seat aircraft on 11 May 1948 wearing the Class-B marks *G.15-5*, MJ276 was delivered to the RIAF on 29 September 1948.

MJ276 was allocated to the Advanced Flying School (AFS) at Ambala Air Force Base, India, in 1949 and assigned the RIAF serial HS537. She remained in RIAF service until 1953 when she was struck off charge and is believed to have been broken up.

MJ451 (HS538)

One of the thousands of Spitfires to be built at the Castle Bromwich factory near Birmingham, MJ451 emerged as an LF Mk.IX before dispatch to 39 MU at Colerne on 8 November 1943 and subsequently to 411 Aircraft Repair Flight (ARF) on 19 November 1943.

MJ451 was allocated to 443 (Hornet) Sqn. RCAF on 13 March 1944 at RAF Ford, West Sussex. She then moved to 341 (Alsace) Sqn., one of the Free French squadrons within the RAF, at Tangmere on 15 June 1944 before passing to 84 Group Support Unit (GSU) of the Second Tactical Air Force (2nd TAF) on 21 July 1944. A week later, on 27 July 1944, MJ451 was allocated to 34 Wing, Servicing Unit Preparation Flight.

The records are somewhat unclear at this point; MJ451 may have been assigned to 38 Sqn. on 4 January 1945. However, on 19 February 1945, she is recorded as

suffering Cat.Ac damage, meaning the repairs were beyond the unit's capability. The official records are unclear who carried out the repair work.

Sold back to her original manufacturer, Vickers-Armstrongs Ltd., on 30 October 1946, MJ451 was converted to Spitfire Trainer configuration at Eastleigh as part of the order for the Royal Indian Air Force (RIAF). Flying as a two-seat aircraft for the first time on 26 May 1948 wearing the Class-B marks *G.15-6*, MJ451 was delivered to the RIAF during September 1948.

Allocated the RIAF serial HS538, MJ451 was allocated to the Advanced Flying School (AFS) at Ambala Air Force Base, India, in 1949 along with the majority of Spitfire Trainers in RIAF service. Struck off charge in 1953, MJ451 was broken up.

MJ518 (HS539)

MJ518 was built as an LF Mk.IX with a Merlin 66 engine at the Castle Bromwich factory; she was taken on charge by the RAF and delivered to 33 MU at RAF Lyneham on 22 November 1943.

She was allocated to 340 (Île-de-France) Sqn. at RAF Perranporth, Cornwall on 7 February 1944 where she was given the codes *GW-W*. MJ518 joined the squadron around the same time as MJ177 *(see MJ177)* which was also later converted to two-seat configuration for the

RIAF. Due to bad weather in the area, the first operational flight with the squadron was not until 13 February when Lt. J. Hommolle piloted MJ518 within Green section on a Convoy Patrol to the south-west of Plymouth, without incident.

MJ518 passed to 84 Group Support Unit (GSU) of the Second Tactical Air Force (2nd TAF) on 13 July 1944, before allocation to 414 Sqn. RCAF on 6 August when the squadron converted from North American P-51 Mustangs. The squadron moved into France, initially to B.21 Advanced Landing Ground (ALG) at Sainte-Honorine, west of Falaise and then B.26 ALG at Illiers-l'Évêque, approximately 40km north of Chartres.

MJ518 is recorded as suffering Cat.Ac damage on 2 November 1944, which may have been the result of flak, but this is not clear. The next mention within the official records for MJ518 is on 3 February 1945 when she arrived at Air Service Training, Hamble.

Sold to Vickers-Armstrongs Ltd., on 30 November 1946, MJ518 was converted to Spitfire Trainer configuration

for the Royal Indian Air Force (RIAF). Flying for the first time on 11 May 1948 as a two-seat aircraft wearing the Class-B marks *G.15-7*, MJ518 was delivered to the RIAF during November 1948. MJ518 was allocated the serial HS539 in RIAF service.

MJ518 was allocated to the Advanced Flying School (AFS) at Ambala Air Force Base, India, in 1949 providing dual instruction for pilots converting to Spitfire Mk.XVIII and Tempest II aircraft. In January 1953 MJ518 moved to the Conversion Training Unit at Hakimpet, near Hyderabad where she remained until the unit converted to Vampires in December of the same year.

It is understood that MJ518 was broken up following her retirement from the RIAF.

However, the surviving substantial fuselage remains of MJ518 (HS539), including the all-important Frame 5 firewall, are in storage with long-term plans to commission a full restoration to airworthy condition and provide a Spitfire Trainer for the Indian Historic Flight, based at Palam Air Force Base near Delhi.

MJ518 (HS539) at Hakimpet Air Force Base during 1952. *(Image: Jagan Pillarisetti via Peter Arnold)*

MK172 (HS540)

MK172 was another of the over 12,000 Spitfires built at Castle Bromwich. Following acceptance by the RAF, MK172 was delivered to 6 MU at RAF Brize Norton on 20 January 1944.

An allocation to 485 (NZ) Sqn. occurred on 11 February 1944 at RAF Hornchurch, when the squadron re-equipped with brand-new Mk.IX Spitfire aircraft. During her 485 Sqn. service MK172 was given the codes *OU-C*. The next official record for MK172 is her arrival at Rolls Royce, Hucknall on 27 May 1944, potentially for testing or trials. Around a year later, on 24 May 1945, she was allocated to the Central Fighter Establishment (CFE) at RAF Tangmere, West Sussex.

MK172 was sold to Vickers-Armstrongs Ltd., on 21 October 1946, and subsequently converted to Spitfire Trainer configuration as part of the order for the Royal Indian Air Force (RIAF). She flew as a two-seat aircraft for the first time on 24 May 1948 wearing the Class-B marks *G.15-8*. MK172 was subsequently delivered to the RIAF on 15 November 1948 and was allocated serial HS540.

MK172 was allocated to the Advanced Flying School (AFS) at Ambala Air Force Base in 1949 along with her fellow Spitfire Trainers in RIAF service. Struck off charge in 1953, MK172 is believed to have been broken up.

MK176 (HS541)

Built at the Castle Bromwich factory as an LF Mk.IX aircraft, MK176 was accepted by the RAF and delivered to 6 MU at Brize Norton on 29 January 1944.

MK176 did not serve with any RAF squadron, she was however dispatched to Flight Refuelling Ltd at RAF Ford, West Sussex on 11 February 1944. A few weeks later, on 29 February, MK176 was allocated to No. 17 Armament Practice Camp at RAF Southend, Essex. She suffered Cat.Ac damage on 3 July 1944, with the repairs being undertaken on site. Her final assignment within the RAF was on 5 October 1946 when MK176 arrived at the Fighter Leaders School, RAF Milfield, Northumberland.

Sold to Vickers-Armstrongs on 24 October 1946, MK176 was converted to Spitfire Trainer configuration as part of the order for the Royal Indian Air Force (RIAF). She flew on 24 May 1948 for the first time as a two-seat aircraft wearing the Class-B marks *G.15-9*. Allocated the serial HS541, MK176 was delivered to the RIAF on 15 November 1948.

Allocated to the Advanced Flying School (AFS) at Ambala Air Force Base, India, in 1949, MK176 served alongside the other Spitfire Trainers. Struck off charge with the RIAF in 1953, the fate of MK176 is unknown, but she is believed to have been broken up.

MK298 (HS542)

MK298 was yet another Spitfire built at the Castle Bromwich aircraft factory outside Birmingham. She was taken on charge by the RAF and delivered to 39 Maintenance Unit (MU) at Colerne, Wiltshire on 4 February 1944.

She was assigned to 329 (Cigognes) Free French Sqn. at RAF Perranporth, Cornwall on 29 February 1944, as part

of a replacement for the squadron's existing Spitfire Mk.V aircraft for brand-new Mk.IXs. MK298 was allocated the codes *5A-W* whilst in service with the squadron. The day after D-Day, on 7 June 1944, she suffered Cat.Ac damage (beyond the capability of the unit to repair) which brought her time with 329 Sqn. to an end.

MK298 was subsequently repaired and then assigned to 341 (Alsace) Sqn., another of the Free French squadrons within the RAF, based at Funtingdon, West Sussex on 22 June 1944. Around 11 August 1944, MK298 moved to 322 (Dutch) Sqn. at RAF Deanland, an Advanced Landing Ground (ALG), west of Hailsham, East Sussex when their existing Spitfire Mk.XIV aircraft were replaced with Mk.IX examples. She suffered Cat.Ac damage on 5 September 1944 which was repaired on site. She was then dispatched to 222 MU at RAF High Ercall, Shropshire on 11 December 1944 for a short period of storage before allocation to the Flight Leaders School, part of the Central Flying School, based at RAF Tangmere, West Sussex on 10 May 1945.

MK298 was sold back to Vickers-Armstrongs on 31 October 1946 and converted to Spitfire Trainer configuration at Eastleigh as part of the order for the Royal Indian Air Force (RIAF). Flying for the first time as a two-seat aircraft on 24 May 1948 wearing the Class-B marks *G.15-10*, MK298 was allocated the serial HS542 and delivered to the RIAF on 15 November 1948.

MK298 was allocated to the Advanced Flying School (AFS) at Ambala Air Force Base, India, in 1949 providing dual instruction for pilots converting to Spitfire Mk.XVIII and Tempest II aircraft. In January 1953 MK298, along with MJ518 and ML417, was re-assigned to the Conversion Training Unit at Hakimpet, near Hyderabad where she remained until the unit converted to Vampires in December of the same year and she was then struck off charge.

It is believed that MK298 was broken up, but this is not confirmed.

A rare image showing MK298 (HS542) along with another unidentified Spitfire Trainer (either MJ518 or ML417) at Hakimpet Air Force Base during 1953. Note the top of the large individual letter/number identifiers which are partially obscured by the starboard wings. HS542 may potentially be '51'. *(Image: Jagan Pillarisetti)*

ML417 marked as *21-T* with 443 (Hornet) Sqn. RCAF in Normandy during summer 1944. *(Image: Peter Arnold collection)*

ML417 (HS543)

ML417 was built at Castle Bromwich before being taken on charge by the RAF and delivered to 6 MU at Brize Norton on 28 April 1944. She passed to 84 Group Support Unit (GSU) of the Second Tactical Air Force (2nd TAF) on 30 May 1944 before being allocated to 443 (Hornet) Sqn. RCAF at RAF Ford, West Sussex and being given the squadron codes *21-T*.

443 Sqn. were kept busy providing low-level fighter cover during the D-Day landings on 6 June 1944. On 15 June, the squadron moved to Sainte-Croix-sur-Mer in Normandy, from where they undertook armed reconnaissance and ground attack missions in the support of the Allied advance through France.

On 26 June 1944, ML417 claimed a damaged/probable Fw190 with pilot Flt. Lt. W.A. Prest at the controls. She then suffered damage following a forced landing at Sainte-Croix-sur-Mer on 3 July and was quickly repaired because on 9 July ML417 was back in the air on a mission over Falaise and suffered flak damage, which was repaired at the squadron. ML417 was flying again by 13 July 1944 with Flt. Lt. W.A. Prest in the cockpit once more, when a Bf109 was claimed as damaged/probable over Alençon, Normandy. Suffering undercarriage damage on 7 August

1944, ML417 was repaired by 410 Repair & Salvage Unit (RSU) before returning to 443 Sqn. on 12 August 1944.

The squadron moved to Illiers-l'Évêque, also in Normandy, on 23 August 1944, before moving once more to B-68 ALG at Le Culot in Belgium (now Beauvechain Air Base). On 20 September F/O R.A. Hodgins claimed two Bf109s destroyed whilst flying ML417, but she also suffered damage (Cat.Ac) during the encounter and was dispatched to 410 RSU once again for repair.

Allocated to 126 Wing, Second Tactical Air Force (2nd TAF) on 5 October 1944, ML417 was assigned to 442 (Caribou) Sqn. RCAF. The Canadian theme continued when on 12 October she moved to 401 (Ram) Sqn. RCAF, then back to 442 Sqn. on 8 March 1945.

RCAF service for ML417 carried on when she was transferred to 441 (Silver Fox) Sqn. on 5 April 1945, then back to 442 Sqn. followed by 412 (Falcon) Sqn. before being allocated to 411 (Grizzly Bear) Sqn. on 29 June 1945. The war in Europe now over, ML417 was dispatched to 29 MU at High Ercall, Shropshire during August 1945 for storage.

ML417 / *G.15-11* at Eastleigh during conversion to Trainer configuration, late 1948. *(Image: Peter Arnold collection)*

ML417 was sold back to Vickers-Armstrongs on 31 October 1946 and converted to Type 509 Spitfire Trainer configuration as part of the order for the Royal Indian Air Force (RIAF). Complete, ML417 flew for the first time in this configuration wearing the Class-B marks *G.15-11* before delivery to the RIAF on 15 November 1948. She was allocated the serial HS543 in RIAF service.

Group Captain Harjinder Singh's first solo flight on 12 July 1950 in ML417/HS543. Grp. Cp., later AVM, Singh was one of the major forces behind the creation of the modern Indian Air Force and the 'father' of the IAF Historic Flight at Delhi. *(Image: AVM Harjinder Singh collection via Mike Edwards)*

HS543 (ML417) in the IAF museum compound at Palam during 1967. Note ill-fitting Griffon engine cowling. *(Image: Peter Arnold collection)*

ML417 was allocated to the Advanced Flying School (AFS) at Ambala Air Force Base, India, in 1949 providing dual instruction for pilots converting to Spitfire and Tempest aircraft. In January 1953 HS543 had moved to Hakimpet, outside Hyderabad, and the resident Conversion Training Unit, where she remained until the unit converted to Vampires in December of the same year.

HS543 (ML417) in a dismantled state, at Overland Park, Kansas during November 1972. She is shown sitting on a trailer owned by Jack Arnold which would normally be used to transport his own Spitfire (Mk.XIV TZ138). Note the project retains the Griffon engine top cowling, visible here in the right foreground. *(Image: Peter Arnold collection)*

ML417 on her first flight following rebuild, at Booker on 10 February 1984. *(Image: Peter Arnold)*

Transferred to the Indian Air Force (IAF) museum at Palam in 1966 for display purposes, HS543 was stored within the museum compound.

Acquired by American Senator Norman E. Gaar on 23 April 1971, HS543 was shipped from Bombay and arrived in Charleston, South Carolina USA on 15 March 1972. Arriving in Overland Park, Kansas on 27 April 1972, little work was carried out before she was sold once more, this time to Stephen Grey in June 1980, when HS543 crossed the Atlantic to *Personal Plane Services* at Booker Airfield arriving on 7 August.

ML417 as a single-seat aircraft once more, and fresh from the paint shop wearing 443 Sqn. RCAF markings at the North Weald Fighter Meet Airshow, on 30 June 1984. Note clipped wing tips. *(Image: Peter Arnold)*

ML417 seen here on 4 May 2018 attending the annual Planes of Fame Airshow at Chino Airport, California. Note full-span wings now fitted. *(Image: John Sanderson)*

At this time the tie-up between the Indian Air Force serial and the original RAF identity had been lost and the RAF serial of the aircraft was unknown. During the rebuild co-author Peter Arnold recommended drilling off the firewall data plate, applied by Vickers when she was converted to two-seat configuration, to see if there was anything on the reverse.

'ML417' was discovered written on the back of the plate and her identity was confirmed once again *(for more information about the confusing world of Spitfire construction numbers see Appendix piece of the same name)*.

Her new owner decided that ML417 was to revert to single-seat configuration and restoration work got underway. ML417 was registered as G-BJSG on 29

January 1981 and she flew once again as a single-seat aircraft on 10 February 1984.

Interestingly, the now surplus two-seat structure removed from ML417 during the rebuild was later incorporated into MH367, now flying in New Zealand *(see MH367)*.

ML417 emerged from rebuild wearing her 443 (Hornet) Sqn. RCAF colours as *2I-T* once more. She was based with the rest of her owner's aeroplanes, *The Fighter Collection*, at Duxford Airfield in Cambridgeshire until ML417 was sold to *Comanche Fighters* and subsequently transported to Texas in December 2001. In the United States she was registered as N2TF.

EGYPT

A single Mk.IX Spitfire Trainer aircraft is documented to have been purchased by the Royal Egyptian Air Force (REAF). Whilst there are reports of a second, and possibly third, Spitfire Trainer aircraft being supplied to the REAF there is no conclusive evidence to confirm these assertions.

RAF Serial	*Class B Marks*	*REAF Serial*
ML113	*G.15-92*	*684*

ML113 (684)

ML113 was built at the Castle Bromwich shadow factory, near Birmingham as an LF Mk.IX fitted with a Merlin 66 engine. She was taken on charge by the RAF and delivered to 39 MU at Colerne on 13 April 1944. Allocated to 308 (City of Kraków) Sqn., ML113 arrived at Chailey Advanced Landing Ground, East Sussex on 3 May 1944. She became the regular mount of Sqn. Ldr. W. Retinger and took part in several Ramrod missions escorting short-range bombers to northern Europe targeting ground targets.

A move to 412 (Falcon) Sqn. RCAF, part of 126 Wing Second Tactical Air Force (2nd TAF), is recorded on 13 July 1944. However, this date must be incorrect as ML113 is recorded as flying operations with the squadron from 3 July 1944. This is no doubt a paperwork issue with a delay getting the aircraft movement card updated. The squadron was based in France at the time and ML113 was kept extremely busy, being the regular aircraft flown by Flt. Lt. R.I. Smith. She has sixty-two (62) missions recorded in the squadron Operations Record Books (ORB), with up to four on some days. ML113 is recorded as suffering Cat.Ac damage, meaning the repairs were beyond the unit's capability, on 16 August 1944.

Whilst there are no details of her repairs, ML113 was subsequently assigned to 411 (Grizzly Bear) Sqn. RCAF on 28 September 1944 and flew two patrol missions. A further move occurred, on 5 October 1944, when ML113 was transferred to 132 (Bombay) Sqn. at RAF Hawkinge, Kent. Five days later, on 10 October, ML113 suffered Cat.Ac damage once more and was repaired on site. ML113's final assignment within the RAF was to the Fighter Command Communication Squadron on 8 July 1945.

Purchased back from the RAF by Vickers-Armstrongs on 16 April 1947, ML113 was converted to Spitfire Trainer configuration, allocated a new construction number (6S/735189), and assigned Class B markings *G.15-92*. She was later registered as G-ALJM and undertook a sales demonstration tour of Scandinavia in October 1949, when Vickers chief test pilot Jeffrey Quill and P.G. Roberts flew her to Copenhagen, Denmark where they arrived on 12 October before flying on to Gothenburg (Göteborg) in Sweden, and eventually arriving in Oslo, Norway on 18 October 1949.

Subsequently sold to the Royal Egyptian Air Force (REAF) on 13 April 1950, ML113 was allocated the REAF serial *684*. Details of her REAF service are sparse, but it is known that ML113 was assigned to the Flying Training School/Advanced Training Squadron (FTS/AFS) at Almaza Air Force Base, located to the north-east of Cairo, Egypt, from April 1950. The fate of ML113 is unknown, but it is believed she was broken up after being struck off charge.

Note: Other sources have erroneously identified this aircraft as RAF serial *'MJ113'*, however this was not issued and falls between serial blocks MH970-MH999 and MJ114-MJ156.

ML113 (G-ALJM) pictured here at Kastrup airport in Copenhagen, Denmark, during a sales tour of Scandinavia in October 1949. Note Danish Air Force Spitfire Mk.IX *430* (RAF serial TD362) in the background. *(Image: Peter Arnold collection)*

ML113 marked as REAF *684*, prior to delivery to Egypt. Note long-range slipper tank fitted. *(Image: Vickers)*

A second Spitfire Trainer for Egypt?

Whilst there is no definitive documentation available, it has been reported via several former pilots that the Royal Egyptian Air Force was supplied with more than one Spitfire Trainer aircraft.

The aircraft shown below, G.15-75, is a previously unknown and undocumented conversion. This has led rise to confusion regarding the aircraft identity, i.e. which RAF serial.

Co-author Peter Arnold walks us through this conundrum and provides a wealth of supporting material in an investigative piece to be found in the Appendix entitled 'An Egyptian Mystery'.

Previously unknown Spitfire Trainer G.15-75 which may have gone to the Egyptian Air Force. *(Image: Phil Jarrett collection via Peter Arnold)*

IRELAND

The Irish Air Corps (IAC) expressed interest and requested a demonstration of a two-seat Spitfire. The prototype Mk.VIII Trainer G-AIDN (MT818) was flown across to Baldonnel, Ireland in June 1950 and conducted a full demonstration to the IAC.

A resulting order for six (6) Type 509 Spitfire Mk.IX Trainer aircraft was subsequently placed by the IAC at a total cost of £71,502, which whilst it included the aircraft, did not include the armament. The order did however include rocket-projectile equipment, recording cameras, a turret sight in the rear cockpit, and 50-gallon torpedo tanks. Additionally, there is mention of the Rolls-Royce Merlin engines installed in the aircraft being overhauled *"to give a life of 400 hours"*.

The aircraft were all delivered to the IAC at Baldonnel by 30 July 1951.

Of the six (6) aircraft supplied to the Irish Air Corps, five (5) survive today.

RAF Serial	Class B Marks	RIAF Serial
MJ627	G.15-171	IAC No.158
MJ772	G.15-172	IAC No.159
MK721	G.15-173	IAC No.160
PV202	G.15-174	IAC No.161
ML407	G.15-175	IAC No.162
TE308	G.15-176	IAC No.163

Superb period image over Baldonnel during the 1950s, featuring ML407 (IAC 162) with MJ772 (IAC 159) and TE308 (IAC 163) captured from the rear seat of another unidentified Spitfire Trainer aircraft. Note the mix of schemes, with IAC 162 wearing all-over silver and 159 & 163 in all-over green, albeit with differing Celtic-boss roundels. *(Image: Stewart Waring via Peter Arnold collection)*

MJ627 over Biggin Hill, 22 May 2019. *(Image: Richard Paver)*

MJ627 (IAC 158)

MJ627 was accepted by the RAF and arrived at 9 MU, RAF Cosford on 4 December 1943, having been built at the Castle Bromwich factory, outside Birmingham. She remained in storage until undergoing preparative work in advance of her allocation to 441 (Silver Fox) Sqn. RCAF, wearing codes *9G-Q,* on 25 September 1944. The squadron was based at the Advanced Landing Ground B-70 near Antwerp, Belgium (now Antwerp International Airport).

MJ627 when in service with 441 Sqn., RCAF, circa 1944. *(Image: Sid Bregman via Peter Arnold collection)*

Two days later, on 27 September 1944, P/O Sid Bregman was flying MJ627 on patrol in the area around Arnhem in the Netherlands when he fell behind the rest of his squadron due to issues with a long-range fuel tank. It was then that P/O Bregman encountered a lone Bf109 which he engaged and managed to down, with the aircraft crashing into the Rhine. This kill was captured by the on-board gun camera, and the footage survives to this day.

MJ627 travelled with the squadron when they were posted to RAF Skeabrae, Orkney on 30 December 1944 to defend the Naval fleet. Whilst at Skeabrae, on 9 March 1945, following a routine patrol, MJ627 suffered engine problems resulting in a forced landing into some heather. This incident was classified as a Cat.E accident (write-off) but the damage was later downgraded to Cat.B (beyond repair on site) on 11 September and she was dispatched to Air Service Training (AST) at Hamble for repair.

With repairs complete, MJ627 was dispatched to 29 MU at RAF High Ercall, Shropshire in late February 1946 to enter a period of storage. Here MJ627 remained until 19 July 1950 when she was declared 'non-effective stock' and sold back to Vickers. A total of two hundred and forty-five (245) flying hours were recorded to this point.

Converted by Vickers to Type 509 two-seat specification, and subsequently sold to the Irish Air Corps (IAC), MJ627 flew for the first time in this configuration wearing the Class-B marks G.15-171 before delivery to Baldonnel on 5 June 1951. MJ627 was given serial 158 in IAC service and was allocated to the Flying Training School. Retired from active service in April 1960, she remained at Baldonnel as an instructional airframe allocated to the Technical Training squadron. A total of 1,036 flying hours had been recorded

Offered for sale during 1961, MJ627 was purchased by John Crewdson/Film Aviation Services Ltd. and arrived at Biggin Hill by road on 13 November 1963. Stored in a dismantled state, MJ627 was registered as G-ASOZ on 19 February 1964. Purchased by Tim Davies as a spares source for his single-seat Spitfire MH434, MJ627 was transported to Elstree and stored. When MJ627 was collected from Biggin Hill her wings and those of MJ772 (IAC 159) were exchanged, and they retain these swapped wings to this day. She was then transported to Stockbridge, Hampshire in December 1967 for further storage.

MJ627 (IAC 158) at Baldonnel, wearing the later all-over silver scheme along with the tri-colour Celtic boss roundel. *(Image: Stewart Waring via Peter Arnold Collection)*

MJ627 stored dismantled in the Vendair hangar at Biggin Hill circa 1964. *(Image: Peter Arnold Collection)*

Purchased by Maurice Bayliss on 7 September 1976, restoration to airworthy condition began at Kenilworth, Warwickshire initially and later at Coventry. Registered as G-BMSB on 3 May 1978, MJ627 had her first post-restoration flight on 8 November 1993 in a 441 Sqn. RCAF scheme with codes *9G-P*. Unfortunately, MJ627 suffered a wheels-up landing at Coventry on 25 April 1998 and was subsequently repaired by a team of volunteers from the *Battle of Britain Memorial Flight* (BBMF), flying once again on 14 February 2002. MJ627 then moved to a new base at Waddington during November 2007.

MJ627 at Duxford Airfield, September 2006. *(Image: Jean-Pierre Touzeau)*

MJ627 at rest, Biggin Hill 27 February 2016. *(Image: John Sanderson)*

Purchased by *Warbird Experiences Ltd.* in April 2014, MJ627 arrived at the *Biggin Hill Heritage Hangar* in December of that year. Since arriving at Biggin Hill, MJ627 has been kept busy providing customer experience flights, being joined by her sister-ships MT818 and MJ772 to make up the trio of airworthy Spitfire Trainer aircraft operated from the *Biggin Hill Heritage Hangar* facility.

MJ627 flying in formation with MJ772 over Biggin Hill during 2019. *(Image: Richard Paver)*

MJ772 airborne over Biggin Hill, 2019. *(Image: Richard Paver)*

MJ772 (IAC 159)

Built as a single-seat LF Mk.IX aircraft with a Rolls-Royce Merlin 66 engine at the Castle Bromwich shadow factory near Birmingham, MJ772 was accepted by the RAF and delivered to 33 MU at RAF Lyneham in December 1943.

Allocated to 341 (Alsace) Sqn., one of the Free French squadrons within the RAF, she arrived on 20 January 1944 at RAF Perranporth. MJ772 was given the squadron codes *NL-W* and took part in operations over Normandy. She suffered a minor landing accident on 18 June 1944 when being flown by Sgt. Dabos, with repairs quickly completed on site.

Days after the completion of the repairs, on 22 June 1944, MJ772 was allocated to another Free-French squadron, 340 (Île-de-France) at RAF Funtington with the codes *GW-A*. She accompanied the squadron in moves to RAF Selsey, RAF Tangmere and later in August 1944 to the Advanced Landing Ground B.8 at Sommervieu, near Bayeaux, Normandy.

By 27 September 1944 MJ772 had been allocated to No.83 G.S.U. (Group Support Unit) at RAF Thorney Island. The main role of this unit was to hold pilots and aircraft in readiness to replace losses in the operational squadrons of the Second Tactical Air Force (2nd TAF). She was eventually allocated to 29 MU (Maintenance Unit) at RAF High Ercall in January 1946 for storage.

MJ772 was sold back to Vickers on 19 July 1950 and converted to Type 509 Spitfire Trainer status at Eastleigh to become part of the order of ten aircraft for the Irish Air Corps. She flew wearing the Class-B marks *G.15-172* in two-seat configuration on 31 May 1951, before being delivered to Baldonnel, Ireland on 5 June 1951.

MJ772 was allocated the IAC serial *158* and, like the other Spitfire Trainer aircraft in IAC service, she was assigned to the Flying Training School. Later, in 1957, she was assigned to A Flight, 1 Sqn. at Baldonnel before allocation to the Technical Training Squadron as an instructional airframe in April 1960.

MJ772 in IAC service at Baldonnel wearing the early two-colour Celtic Boss roundel. *(Image: Peter Arnold collection)*

Offered for sale by the IAC and purchased by John Crewdson/Film Aviation Services Ltd, MJ772 arrived at Biggin Hill on 5 November 1963 and entered a short period of storage in a dismantled state.

She was then sold on to COGEA, who already owned several single-seat Spitfires that towed targets for a NATO armed forces contract. MJ772 arrived via airfreight at their Ostend, Belgium base on 1 April 1964.

It was just before this sale that the wings were swapped between MJ772 and MJ627 *(see MJ627)* and they retain these swapped wings to this day.

MJ772 was shipped back to Elstree in the UK following purchase by Anthony Samuelson/Samuelson's Film Services in 1965 where she underwent a rebuild to airworthy condition by Simpson's Aeroservices Ltd. Following completion of the rebuild, MJ772 flew on 8 November 1966 registered as G-AVAV.

MJ772 in the hangar at Baldonnel. Shown in the early all-over green markings but with the later tri-colour Celtic Boss roundel. Note lack of rear canopy, engine cowlings and wing tip. *(Image: Graham Skillen via Peter Arnold collection)*

MJ772 in the Simpson's Aerospace hangar at Elstree on 12 February 1967. *(Image: Peter Foote via Peter Arnold collection)*

We have been granted special permission to include this personal Samuelson family photograph of MJ772 (G-AVAV) taken at Elstree during 1967. Anthony Samuelson is sitting on the wing with sons Will, Bertie, and Julian. *(Image: Will Samuelson)*

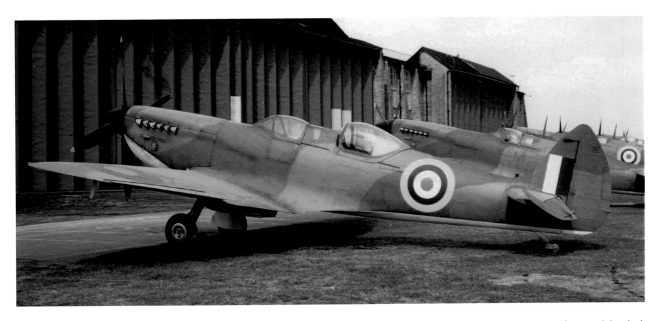

MJ772 at RAF Henlow on 18 April 1968 for *The Battle of Britain* movie press preview. Note incorrect large red centre on the roundels which were all corrected prior to filming. *(Image: Peter Arnold collection)*

She was leased to Spitfire Productions Ltd in mid-1967 for inclusion in the movie *The Battle of Britain* and flown to Henlow in early 1968 to join the fleet of aircraft being used for the film. Repainted in the film colour-scheme to represent the colours worn by 1940-era Spitfire aircraft, MJ772 is known to have worn several different squadron code letters during filming.

MJ772 unfortunately suffered a forced landing at Little Staughton, Bedfordshire on 9 July 1968 due to an engine failure. She ended up on her belly and this signalled the end of her film career. Transported to Duxford and rebuilt by Simpson's Aeroservices Ltd once again, MJ772 was flying by early 1969 when she was delivered back to her owner at Elstree.

Pilot Wilson *'Connie'* Edwards standing on the wing of MJ772 after her forced landing at Little Staughton on 9 July 1968, during filming for the movie *The Battle of Britain*. Note B-25 camera-ship in the background. *(Image: Wilson 'Connie' Edwards via Peter Arnold Collection)*

MJ772 at Elstree in early May 1969 in preparation for the *Daily Mail* London to New York air-race. Note faded *Battle of Britain* film codes CD-N still visible. *(Image: Richard Riding via Peter Arnold collection)*

Owner, Anthony Samuelson, decided to enter the *Daily Mail* London to New York air-race using several of his aircraft, including his Hurricane and Spitfire MJ772. The aircraft left Elstree on 5 May 1969 bound for Ireland, unfortunately MJ772 made a forced landing at RNAS Brawdy in Wales due to fuel issues and was subsequently withdrawn from the race.

Offered for sale, MJ772 was purchased by Sir William J.D. Roberts and flown to Shoreham on 29 April 1970. It was at Shoreham that she received a change of markings, to emerge in 341 (Alsace) Sqn. markings as *NL-R*. Later she was ferried to her owner's Scottish base at Strathallan, arriving on 17 December 1971.

MJ772 on 22 September 1973 at Strathallan in Scotland, wearing 341 (Alsace) Sqn. markings with incorrect brown/green camouflage, it should be grey/green. Note the 'R' for then owner Sir William Roberts. *(Image: Peter Arnold Collection)*

MJ772 with rear cockpit faired over, flying across the German countryside during August 2013. *(Image: Richard Paver)*

Purchased by Doug Champlin/Champlin Fighter Museum, MJ772 departed Scotland on 13 December 1974 bound for Enid, Oklahoma USA. She was registered to her new owner as N8R in May 1975. Bound for Mesa, Arizona, and the museum's new location, MJ772 unfortunately suffered a forced landing at Amarillo, Texas on 22 July 1980 and sustained damage to the underside of the fuselage and wings. Transported to Mesa to conduct the repairs, MJ772 was airworthy once again by October 1985. In addition to the repair work, the opportunity was taken to panel over the rear cockpit to resemble a single-seat Mk.IX Spitfire. The front cockpit was not altered in any way which meant that it remained 13½ inches further forward than a standard single-seat aircraft, giving MJ772 a rather unique look.

MJ772 remained on display within the Champlin Fighter Museum until 2000 when the entire collection was sold to The Museum of Flight, Seattle. With the Museum already having a Spitfire on display within their collection, MJ772 was loaned to the Experimental Aircraft Association (EAA) for display in their museum at Oshkosh, Wisconsin, where she arrived on 14 April 2004.

She was purchased by Volker Schulke/Air Fighter Academy in late 2010 and transported to *Meier Motors*, Bremgarten, Germany for a return to airworthy condition and was registered as D-FMKN. Following her return to flight, MJ772 was flown to her owner's base at Heringsdorf, on the island of Usedom in Germany. On 15 September 2015, whilst flying to Goodwood Aerodrome, MJ772 suffered an engine failure and subsequently made a forced landing in a field near Ashford, Kent. She was transported to the *Biggin Hill Heritage Hangar* and stored.

MJ772 was acquired by *Warbird Experiences Ltd*, the operator already offering customer experience flights in two-seat Spitfires MT818 and MJ627 at Biggin Hill. A full programme of work was undertaken to return MJ772 to airworthy condition, with a first post-rebuild flight on 26 February 2019. She emerged in the colours of 341 (Île-de-France) Sqn. with the codes *GW-A* to reflect the markings worn whilst serving with the squadron during 1944.

Based at Biggin Hill, MJ772 is currently one of three airworthy Spitfire Trainer aircraft on site, along with MT818 and MJ627, offering customer experience flights.

MJ772 over Germany with rear cockpit back in use once more, 15 May 2014. *(Image: Richard Paver)*

MJ772 under rebuild at the *Biggin Hill Heritage Hangar* facility, October 2018. *(Image: Fred Mussard)*

MK721 (IAC 160)

Built at the Castle Bromwich shadow-factory, MK721 was taken on charge by the RAF and delivered to 6 MU at RAF Brize Norton on 31 March 1944.

Allocated to 401 (City of Westmount) Sqn. RCAF at RAF Tangmere, MK721 had her first mission with the squadron on 30 June 1944 when she was part of a dive-bombing patrol, carrying 500lb bombs. Life for MK721 was extremely busy within the squadron with a mix of armed-recce and patrol sorties, sometimes with up to three or four missions a day.

On 7 June 1944, the day following the D-Day landings in Normandy and with pilot F/O E.T. Gardner at the controls, MK721 was on a mission to the Mézidon area, south-east of Caen when she was forced to return to base due to radio trouble. With Flt. Lt. R.R. Bouskill in the cockpit, one of MK721's regular pilots, she was part of a flight of aircraft from 401 Sqn. on an armed recce mission in the Mortain/Vitré/Laval area of Normandy on 3 August 1944. The squadron encountered several enemy aircraft with Flt. Lt. Bouskill managing to destroy one Bf109 during the skirmish before all aircraft safely returned to base.

MK721 accompanied 401 Squadron when they moved from Tangmere to the B.4 Advanced Landing Ground (ALG) at Bény-sur-Mer, north of Caen, on 8 August 1944 as part of the Allied advance into mainland Europe.

Following the war MK721 was sold back to Vickers for conversion to Type 509 two-seat trainer configuration on 19 July 1950. Flying for the first time as a two-seat aircraft on 19 June 1951 with the Class-B marks *G.15-173*, MK721 was taken on charge by the IAC on 29 June 1951 when she was flown to Baldonnel, Ireland, marked as IAC 160.

Unfortunately, MK721 was involved in a crash upon landing at Baldonnel on 15 February 1957 which was classified as a Cat.E2 incident meaning the aircraft was a write-off and she was subsequently struck off charge. Her shaken pilot survived the incident and following his time with the IAC went on to enjoy a career flying for the Irish airline *Aer Lingus*.

The battered wreck of MK721 ended up on the airfield dump at Baldonnel where she remained for some time before being transported to a local scrapyard where she was then broken up.

Nothing remains of MK721 today.

A rare image of MK721 (IAC 160) at Baldonnel. *(Image: Jim Masterson via Peter Arnold Collection)*

Superb image of PV202 wearing early IAC colours. Pilot John Romain with legendary Spitfire test-pilot Alex Henshaw in the rear cockpit, flying over Duxford Airfield, 23 March 2005. *(Image: Richard Paver)*

PV202 (IAC 161)

Built at the Castle Bromwich shadow factory as an LF Mk.IXe, PV202 was taken on charge by the RAF and delivered to 33 MU at Lyneham, Wiltshire on 18 September 1944. She was allocated to 84 Ground Support Unit (GSU) at Thruxton on 8 October 1944, and then only ten days later, on 19 October, PV202 was transferred to 33 Sqn., 135 Wing, Second Tactical Air Force (2nd TAF). The squadron was at the time based at B-51 Advanced Landing Ground (ALG), which is now Lille Airport, France. PV202 was allocated the squadron codes *5R-Q*.

33 Sqn. moved to B-65 ALG at Maldegem, Belgium where PV202 continued to carry out sorties through to December 1944 before another move brought the aircraft back to the UK on 15 December.

During her service with 33 Sqn., PV202 is known to have flown twenty operational sorties with ten different pilots from Great Britain, Denmark, the Netherlands, and South Africa. On her return to the UK, PV202 went to 84 GSU, now at Lasham in Hampshire, before transfer to 83 GSU at Dunsfold, Surrey on 20 January 1945.

Allocated to 412 (Falcon) Sqn. RCAF on 25 January 1945 and initially issued codes *VZ-M*, then later *VZ-W*, PV202 joined the squadron at B-88 ALG at Heesch in the Netherlands. On 17 March 1945, PV202 and pilot P/O H.W. Grant downed a Fw190 whilst on a dive-bombing mission. Another aircraft fell to PV202's guns on 25 March 1945, when Sqn. Ldr. M.D. Boyd downed a Bf109.

The squadron had moved to B-116 ALG at Wunstorf, Germany by 16 April 1945, and it was whilst she was flying from here on 29 April with Flt. Lt. J.H. Maclean at the controls, PV202 downed yet another Fw190. 412 Sqn. returned to the UK, and Dunsfold, in May 1945 with PV202 subsequently allocated to 83 GSU once more on 31 May. Flown to 29 MU at High Ercall on 29 July 1945, she then entered a period of storage.

PV202 was sold to Vickers-Armstrongs on 19 July 1950 and converted to Type 509 two-seat Trainer configuration for the Irish Air Corps (IAC). She was flight tested from Eastleigh wearing Class-B marks *G.15-174* and was delivered to the IAC at Baldonnel, Ireland, on 29 June 1951.

PV202 (IAC 161) upon delivery to the Irish Air Corps at Baldonnel, wearing early all-over green scheme with two-colour Celtic Boss roundel. *(Image: Peter Arnold collection)*

PV202 was allocated the IAC serial *161* and served alongside the other Spitfire Trainer aircraft in IAC service at the Flying Training School, Baldonnel. On 4 December 1960, she was assigned to the Technical Training Squadron as an instructional airframe. Struck off charge in February 1960, PV202 was offered for sale.

PV202 (IAC 161) in later all-over silver scheme & tri-colour Celtic Boss roundel, at Baldonnel. *(Image: Peter Arnold Collection)*

PV202 in flight on 29 April 1990, shortly after her return to airworthy condition. *(Image: Hugh Smallwood via Peter Arnold Collection)*

PV202 was purchased by Anthony Samuelson (Samuelson's Film Services), along with sister-ships ML407/IAC 162 and airworthy TE308/IAC 163 on 4 March 1968. Both PV202 and ML407 were transported to Cricklewood, North London and placed in storage. Both stored aircraft were subsequently acquired by Sir William J.D. Roberts in April 1970 and initially transported to Flimwell, and later Shoreham, before going to their owner's Scottish base at Strathallan, where they arrived on 2 March 1972. Stored in a dismantled state, PV202 remained at Strathallan until 9 August 1979 when she was sold to E.N. Grace (along with ML407/IAC 162) at St. Merryn in Cornwall, before being sold on to S.W. Atkins on 10 October.

PV202 was initially registered as G-BHGH, before being re-registered as G-TRIX on 2 July 1980. Work to return PV202 to airworthy condition was undertaken at several locations before she settled at her owner's workshop in Battle, East Sussex around February 1986. PV202 then moved to BAE Dunsfold during December 1989 in preparation for flight.

PV202 retained her second seat during the rebuild but adopted the lower-profile 'Grace-Melton' canopy configuration (see *ML407*). PV202 underwent a successful first post-restoration flight from Dunsfold on 23 February 1990 in the capable hands of Peter Kynsey, wearing her former 412 Sqn. RCAF colours as *VZ-M*. Ownership then passed to Richard Parker who operated PV202 for a period before selling her to Rick Roberts on 14 February 1992.

Suffering damage caused by an undercarriage issue when landing at her Goodwood base on 16 September 1996, PV202 was shipped to *Hawker Restorations* at Earls Colne for repair work. Emerging from the repairs in a new colour scheme as *5R-Q* of 33 Sqn., another of her former squadrons, PV202 was sold to Greg McCarrach in October 1999. Sadly, both the owner and his flight instructor Norman Lees were killed in an accident whilst flying PV202 at Goodwood on 8 April 2000. The aircraft was written off.

Following the completion of a crash investigation at Farnborough, the remains of PV202 were offered for sale. Purchased by Karol Bos, owner of Historic Flying Ltd. (HFL), PV202 arrived on 28 February 2001 at their Duxford Airfield facility. She was registered as G-CCCA on 18 February 2003.

PV202 in 33 Sqn. markings as *5R-Q*, Duxford Airfield, July 1999. *(Image: Jean-Pierre Touzeau)*

A full restoration back to airworthy condition commenced with the decision being made to revert PV202 back to Vickers Type 509 Trainer configuration and the rear 'bubble' canopy. The original rear cockpit frame from PV202 was found in Norfolk and incorporated into the airframe during the rebuild.

PV202 took to the skies once more with pilot John Romain at the controls on 13 January 2005, wearing the striking early all-over green colour scheme of the Irish Air Corps, as *161*, replicating markings she wore when with the service during the 1950s.

PV202 in early IAC markings as *161*, Duxford Airfield, 11 June 2005. *(Image: John Sanderson)*

PV202 as *H-98*, Duxford Airfield, 24 April 2010. *(Image: John Sanderson)*

In March 2007 PV202 was repainted to represent *'H-98'* *(see BS274)*, one of the three Royal Netherlands Air Force (RNethAF) Spitfire Trainer aircraft.

In May 2010 plans were made to paint PV202 in a *Battle of Britain* (BoB) film livery with codes *AI-E* to partner the *Aeroplane Restoration Company* (ARCo) Hispano Buchon which was also in BoB film markings.

However, after three days of painting, the application submitted to the RAF Events Team via the CAA was unfortunately rejected on the basis that it did not represent a true RAF livery.

PV202 was subsequently coded *QV-I*, a 19 Squadron machine based at Duxford.

We are privileged to be have been granted permission for a 'one off' inclusion of this never seen before image of PV202, taken on 11 May 2010 at Duxford, wearing the very short-lived *AI-E* codes. *(Image: Col Pope)*

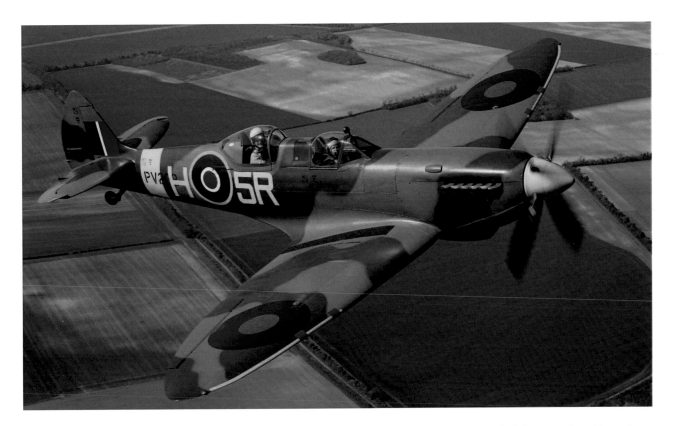

PV202 in 33 Sqn. colours once more. Seen here over Cambridgeshire being flown by Steve Jones on 9 April 2017. *(Image: Harry Measures)*

By mid-2014 PV202 underwent another change of markings, emerging in 33 Sqn. colours once again, but this time with the squadron codes *5R-H*.

Operated under the *Aerial Collective* banner with sister-ship PT462, PV202 is based at historic Duxford Airfield providing customer experience flights.

PV202 at rest with sister-ship PT462 behind. On the flight-line at the Battle of Britain Airshow, Duxford Airfield on 22 September 2018. *(Image: Peter Arnold)*

PV202 wearing a Battle of Britain era 19 Sqn. colour scheme as *QV-1*. Pilot Dave (Rats) Ratcliffe at the controls with Eric Carter, a Force Benedict veteran, in the rear seat flying over Goodwood Aerodrome during the summer of 2011. *(Image: Richard Paver)*

A fine study of ML407 wearing 485 (NZ) Sqn. colours, during 2016. *(Image: Richard Paver)*

ML407 (IAC 162)

Built as an LF Mk.IX at the Castle Bromwich aircraft factory, ML407 was taken on charge by the RAF and delivered to 33 MU at Lyneham, Wiltshire on 23 April 1944 in preparation for squadron service. Allocated to 485 (NZ) Sqn. at Selsey, West Sussex, ML407 was delivered on 29 April 1944. ML407, now coded *OU-V*, became the personal aircraft of F/O Johnnie Houlton

DFC, although she was flown by many of the other squadron pilots.

Due to bad weather ML407's first mission with the squadron on 1 May 1944, escorting Boston bombers, was abandoned and they were all recalled.

ML407 with F/O Johnnie Houlton at the controls, 27 August 1944. *(Image: Peter Arnold collection)*

ML407 was, however, kept busy in the build up to D-Day, flying fighter sweep missions across the English Channel, and escorting medium bombers on raids, along with carrying out a number of bombing missions equipped with a 500lb bomb under the belly of the aircraft.

The squadron moved to B-17 Advanced Landing Ground (ALG), at what is now Caen-Carpiquet Airport, with ML407 arriving on 31 August 1944. The squadron was tasked with providing essential air support to the ground forces. By mid-September 1944, the squadron moved once more. to B-35 ALG, at Eu near Le Tréport. Another move by the end of September, this time to B-53 ALG at Merville, near Lille.

ML407 suffered Cat.Ac damage whilst landing on 12 October 1944, meaning it was beyond the capability of the squadron to repair. She was repaired however, and on 11 December re-joined 485 Sqn., who had now moved to B-65 ALG at Maldegem, near Bruges.

After flying 139 sorties in her eight busy months with 485 Sqn., ML407 was reassigned to 145 Wing, Second Tactical Air Force (2nd TAF) on 28 December 1944 and formally allotted to 341 (Alsace) Sqn. on 4 January 1945 when she was allocated the codes *NL-D*.

There then followed a period of short squadron assignments when on 11 January 1945, ML407 moved to 308 (City of Kraków) Sqn. at B-61 ALG near Ghent in Belgium and was given the codes *ZF-R*. A few weeks later, on 8 February, ML407 was allocated to 349 (Belgian) Sqn. who were stationed at B-77 ALG, Gilze-Rijen, Netherlands and was coded *GE-P*. Then on 22 March 1945, she was assigned to another Free French squadron, 345 Sqn. as *2Y-A* at B-85 ALG, Schijndel, Netherlands.

The final squadron assignment for ML407 came on 19 April 1945 when she was allocated to 332 (Norwegian) Sqn. at B-85 ALG, Schijndel, Netherlands and given the codes *AH-B*. The squadron moved on to B-106 ALG at Twenthe, Netherlands on 21 April 1945, before being withdrawn from operations the next day and deploying to Dyce, Scotland en route home to Norway, but without ML407. ML407 was briefly returned to 485 (NZ) Sqn., also based at Twenthe, before going to 151 Repair Unit at B-55, Wevelgem, Belgium (now Flanders International Airport) on 26 April 1945.

Returning to the UK, she was then placed in storage at 29 MU, High Ercall on 27 September 1945. ML407 was sold to Vickers-Armstrongs Ltd. on 19 July 1950 and converted to Type 509 two-seat Trainer configuration for the Irish Air Corps (IAC).

ML407 at Eastleigh before delivery to the IAC, July 1951. *(Image: Vickers via Peter Arnold collection)*

ML407 (IAC 162) with her crew at Baldonnel. Note the underwing tri-colour markings. *(Image: Peter Arnold collection)*

She was flight tested from Eastleigh wearing Class-B marks *G.15-175* on 24 July 1951 and then delivered to the IAC at Baldonnel, Ireland, on 30 July 1951 where she was given the IAC serial *162* and allocated to B Flight,

Fighter Training School. She was transferred to A Flight, No.1 Sqn., Gormanston on 26 April 1957 for air-to-ground gunnery practice, before returning to the Fighter Training School at Baldonnel again on 28 July 1958.

ML407 with the Technical Training squadron as an instructional airframe at Baldonnel. 29 July 1967. *(Image: R.A. Scholefield)*

The fuselage of ML407 in storage at Shoreham, 3 May 1971. *(Image: Peter Arnold)*

ML407 was assigned to the Technical Training squadron as an instructional airframe on 8 July 1960. Struck off charge in February 1964, ML407 was then offered for sale in a dismantled state.

ML407 was purchased by Anthony Samuelson (Samuelson's Film Services) along with sister-ships PV202/IAC 161 and airworthy TE308/IAC 163 on 4 March 1968. Both ML407 and PV202 were transported to Cricklewood, North London and placed in storage. They were both then acquired by Sir William J.D. Roberts in April 1970 and initially transported to Flimwell and Shoreham before going to their owner's Scottish base at Strathallan, arriving on 2 March 1972. Stored in a dismantled state, both ML407 & PV202 remained at Strathallan until 9 August 1979 when they were sold to Nick Grace and transported to St. Merryn in Cornwall, arriving 29 October.

ML407 undergoing engine runs with Dick Melton at the controls, St Merryn. 15 April 1985. *(Image: Peter Arnold)*

ML407 at Duxford Airfield, September 2006. *(Image: Jean-Pierre Touzeau)*

ML407 was registered as G-LFIX on 1 February 1980 and the process of restoring her to airworthy condition got underway. Whilst the rebuild retained the second cockpit, a new low-profile canopy was installed by owner Nick Grace and ex. *Battle of Britain Memorial Flight* chief engineer Dick Melton which is now known as the 'Grace-Melton' canopy arrangement.

Other Spitfire Trainer rebuilds have since adopted the 'Grace-Melton' style modification *(see PT462, MH367, EN570 and BS548)*.

A first post-restoration flight took place on 16 April 1985 at St. Merryn with owner Nick Grace at the controls and his wife Carolyn in the rear seat, with ML407 wearing just primer and her civil registration. Soon repainted, ML407 was once again wearing her 485 (NZ) Sqn. colours and codes *OU-V*.

Based initially at Middle Wallop, Hampshire, ML407, or the *Grace Spitfire* as she is affectionately known, now divides her time between Sywell Aerodrome in Northamptonshire and Duxford Airfield in Cambridgeshire.

ML407 over Duxford Airfield during 2019. Note undercarriage doors without D-Day stripes. *(Image: Jerry Ridout)*

ML407 showing off her 'Grace-Melton' rear canopy to good effect. Photographed at Sywell on 5 September 2019, she wears 341 Squadron markings as *NL-D*, with whom she flew during December 1944. *(Image: Nigel Harrison)*

Following the tragic death of Nick Grace during 1988 due to a car accident, Carolyn learned to fly the Spitfire and went solo during 1990. Retiring from flying in 2017, Carolyn had amassed over nine hundred (900) hours flying ML407.

The *Grace Spitfire* has been, and still is, extremely active at airshows and events throughout the UK and is now flown by Carolyn's son Richard along with other pilots within the *Ultimate Warbird Flights* team.

ML407 / The *Grace Spitfire* is operated by *Ultimate Warbird Flights* and offers customer experience flights from Sywell Aerodrome, Northamptonshire.

Taken on 7 September 2019, this image of ML407 shows her attending the Air Legend airshow at Melun-Villaroche Airfield, near Paris, France. *(Image: Jean-Pierre Touzeau)*

ML407 being flown by Alex Smee over the Fontainebleau forest, just south of Melun, France on 7 September 2019, wearing authentic 341 (Alsace) Sqn. markings. *(Image: Xavier Meal)*

TE308 over Aspen, Colorado, 22 August 1986. Pilot Bill Greenwood, with Kay Arnold in the back. *(Image: Peter Arnold)*

TE308 (IAC 163)

Built as a low-back, single-seat Spitfire HF Mk.IX (Merlin 70 engine) at Castle Bromwich, TE308 was accepted by the RAF and delivered to 39 MU at Colerne on 9 June 1945.

She remained in storage until 16 January 1950, when she was then transferred to 29 MU at High Ercall, Shropshire.

TE308 in storage with 39 MU at Colerne during 1949. Points to note are TE308's low-back fuselage and clipped wings. *(Image: C. Kinghorn via Peter Arnold Collection)*

Not a good start to her IAC career! TE308's arrival at Baldonnel upon delivery from Vickers, on 30 July 1951, when her undercarriage failed to lock down and she ended up on her belly. *(Image: Peter Arnold collection)*

TE308 was sold back to Vickers-Armstrongs Ltd. on 19 July 1950 *(the same day as PV202)* for conversion to Type 509 two-seat configuration for the Irish Air Corps (IAC). She is unique, however, in that TE308 is the only low-back Spitfire to have undergone conversion to two-seat Trainer status.

TE308 was test flown from Eastleigh wearing Class-B marks *G.15-176* prior to delivery to the IAC at Baldonnel

on 30 July 1951, where she was allocated the IAC serial *163*.

Arriving at Baldonnel along with ML407/IAC 162, TE308 was under the control of pilot Capt. 'Tim' Healy, who after performing a short display over the field, came in for landing, found that the undercarriage had failed to lock down, and suffered a belly-landing.

TE308 in Irish Air Corps service, Baldonnel. Note later style tri-colour Celtic Boss roundel. *(Image: Peter Arnold collection)*

TE308 on 7 May 1968, being collected from Baldonnel, bound for Elstree. *(Image: Peter Sargent via Peter Arnold collection)*

Following repair at a maintenance unit, TE308 was allocated to A Flight, Flying Training School at Baldonnel. She suffered an incident in August 1961 and was grounded, before being allocated to the Technical Training squadron as an instructional airframe in September of the same year. TE308 was offered for sale on 4 March 1968. It can be assumed that the Technical Training squadron kept TE308 in an operational condition due to the short amount of time between being offered for sale and her departure from Baldonnel.

TE308, along with sister-ships PV202 and ML407, was purchased by Anthony Samuelson (Samuelson's Film Services) and subsequently registered as G-AWGB on 4 April 1968, before flying to Elstree on 7 May.

Leased to Spitfire Productions Ltd., TE308 flew to Henlow the following day on 8 May to join the amassing fleet of aircraft for the upcoming movie *The Battle of Britain*.

A unique shot showing the two Spitfire Trainers that participated in the filming of the movie *The Battle of Britain*. TE308 is pictured on the left with a Hispano Buchon propeller, and MJ772 is beyond wearing CD-H codes. Location is likely Debden during June 1968. *(Image: Dave McDonald via Peter Arnold Collection)*

TE308 sporting one of the many fictitious squadron codes worn during the filming of the movie *The Battle of Britain*. Seen here at Duxford on 6 August 1968. Note Hispano Buchon propellor. *(Image: Peter Arnold)*

During the filming, TE308 had a camera fitted in the front cockpit with the pilot flying the aircraft from the rear. She appeared in the film, albeit in the rear of the shot, so the second cockpit would be less noticeable. It is known that TE308 wore at least fourteen unique sets of squadron codes during the filming to give the impression of different aircraft.

With the completion of filming, TE308 was flown to Bovingdon by November 1968, before returning to Elstree, where she joined fellow ex. IAC Spitfire MJ772/IAC 159.

TE308 (G-AWGB) during the filming of *The Battle of Britain* movie at Duxford in August 1968. Note pilot flying aircraft from rear cockpit with camera set up in the front seat position. *(Image: Adrian Balch via Peter Arnold collection)*

Don Plumb, on the left, with Vickers test pilot Dave Morgan at Shoreham on 15 May 1971 for a familiarisation flight in MJ772 prior to the first flight of TE308 in Canada. Dave Morgan served with 617 Sqn. RAF, then transferred to the Fleet Air Arm flying Seafires, before joining Vickers in 1950. *(Image: Peter Arnold)*

Advertised for sale along with MJ772, PV202, ML407, and a Hurricane, they were all purchased by Sir William J.D. Roberts on 20 April 1970. TE308 and MJ772 flew to Shoreham on 1 May 1970 along with the Hurricane.

TE308 was sold to Canadian businessman Don Plumb on 16 July 1970. She left Shoreham on 23rd July for

Borehamwood in preparation for packing ready for shipment on 11 September aboard the ship SS *Wolfgang Russ*. Having safely arrived in Toronto, Canada, on 9 October 1970, TE308 was registered as CF-RAF (later C-FRAF) and transported to Windsor, Ontario for refurbishment and reassembly before her first flight in Canada on 23 July 1971.

TE308 on a test flight out of Windsor, Ontario on 30 July 1971. Don Plumb flying with Jerry Billing in the rear cockpit. *(Image: Peter Arnold Collection)*

Don Plumb flying TE308, now sporting a camouflage scheme, over Lake Ontario in October 1971. *(Image: Peter Arnold collection)*

Initially flown in two-seat configuration, TE308 underwent modification around 1973 to remove the rear canopy and skin over the resulting void. This work was to give an approximate appearance of the single-seat version of the aircraft without moving the front cockpit rearwards 13½ inches to its normal position, resulting in a unique appearance which was later replicated on MJ772, one of the other former IAC Spitfire Trainer aircraft *(see MJ772)*. TE308 was given a green and dark-earth colour scheme along with the spurious squadron codes *RA-F* (port) and *R-AF* (starboard).

Following the tragic death of owner Don Plumb in a crash flying his P-51D during 1975, TE308 was sold to Thomas Watson Jr. Ferried on 1 October 1976 to her new owners base at the Owl's Head Transportation Museum, Owl's Head, Maine by Jerry Billings, TE308 was registered N92477.

TE308 over Ontario in 1973, with Don Plumb at the controls. Note rear cockpit faired over. *(Image: Peter Arnold collection)*

Having been invited to accompany Bill Greenwood on his annual trip to Oshkosh in TE308 from his home base in Aspen Colorado, some 1,250 miles, here Peter Arnold endeavours unsuccessfully to photograph Concorde taking off on 29 July 1990. Thankfully 'a spectator' captured the shot and sent it to Bill who entitled it '*The three British eccentricities*'.

Acquired by Woodson K. Woods of Scottsdale, Arizona on 7 October 1979, TE308 was ferried once more by Jerry Billings to her new owner's base. In Woods' ownership the rear seat was restored and TE308 received a new grey and green colour scheme along with the spurious codes *WK-C* before going on display at the Carefree Aviation Museum near Phoenix, Arizona.

In April 1983 TE308 was sold once more, this time to Bill Greenwood of Aspen, Colorado. By 1994 TE308 was wearing new codes *RJ-M* as a nod to Spitfire designer R.J. Mitchell. In Greenwood's ownership TE308 attended many airshows and events throughout the USA.

TE308 taking off during '*The Gathering of Spitfires*' at Carefree Airport, Arizona on 20 October 1995. *(Image: Peter Arnold)*

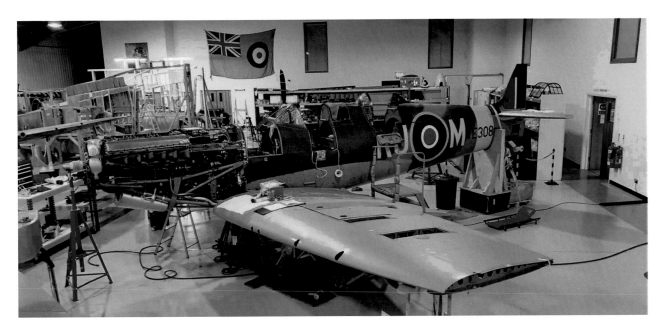

TE308 under rebuild at the *Biggin Hill Heritage Hangar*, 17 March 2020. *(Image: John Sanderson)*

Unfortunately. on 26 April 2008, TE308 suffered a major incident whilst landing at Scholes International Airport, Galveston, Texas. TE308 was unable to avoid a Hawker Hurricane which ground-looped whilst landing ahead of her and both aircraft collided on the runway.

Whilst the incident caused damage to both aircraft, fortunately no one was seriously injured. TE308 was transported to Q.G. Aviation at Fort Collins, Colorado for repair. Some remediation work was carried out, including to the wings and Rolls Royce Merlin engine.

Acquired by the *Biggin Hill Heritage Hangar*, TE308 arrived at Biggin Hill on 21 November 2019. Work is underway to return her to airworthy condition and is progressing at a rapid pace with the wings and engine fitted by 19 February 2020. The plan is to have TE308 flying again during 2020.

TE308 receiving new markings at Biggin Hill, 5 July 2020. Once complete, she will emerge wearing the colours of A58-606 / ZP-W (Note, A58-606 was a Mk.VIII, ex. RAF MT819) of 457 'Grey Nurse' Sqn. Royal Australian Air Force (RAAF), which was the personal aircraft of Sqn. Ldr. Bruce Watson. *(Image: Peter Monk)*

WARBIRD ERA

All orders for Spitfire Trainer aircraft had been fulfilled by the end of July 1951 and eventually all development works were stopped. This was not however, to be the end of the two-seat Spitfire story!

In more recent times, or the *Warbird-era*, a resurgence of interest from owners, investors and engineers alike have resulted in several Spitfire aircraft being rebuilt to two-seat Trainer configuration with the promise of yet more to come.

In this chapter we present a detailed history for each of the aircraft which have flown following a *Warbird-era* rebuild or conversion to two-seat configuration.

RAF Serial	*Civil Reg*	*Notes*
PT462	G-CTIX	*First flight – 25 July 1987*
MH367	ZK-WDQ	*First flight – 16 September 2006*
SM520	G-ILDA	*First flight – 17 October 2008*
NH341	G-CICK	*First flight – 11 March 2017*

Three Spitfire Mk.IX Trainer aircraft tucked up safely in the hangar at Sywell Aerodrome, Northamptonshire on 15 August 2017. Aircraft are, from left to right, NH341, ML407 and PV202. *(Image: Aero Legends)*

Pilot Steve Jones flying PT462 over Cambridgeshire on 9 June 2018. *(Image: Harry Measures)*

PT462

Built at the Castle Bromwich shadow factory as a HF Mk.IXe fitted with a Merlin 70 engine, PT462 was dispatched to 39 MU at RAF Colerne on 21 July 1944. She then underwent a further move to 215 MU at RAF Dumfries on 31 July 1944 for packing prior to shipment to the Mediterranean Allied Air Forces aboard the ship *Silver Sandal* on 9 August. She arrived in Casablanca, Morocco on 23 August 1944.

PT462 was allocated to 4 Sqn. SAAF, coded *KJ-Z*, from 19 November 1944 and took part in operations around the Adriatic and Balkans region during this time. In April 1945 she served with 253 Sqn. RAF, coded *SW-A*, and took part in operations over Yugoslavia.

Post-war, PT462 was declared surplus by the RAF, sold to the Italian Air Force (IAF) on 26 June 1947 and allocated the IAF serial MM4100. She was assigned to 5° Stormo at Orio al Serio, east of Milan in December 1947.

Following a period in storage, PT462 was part of a batch of Spitfire aircraft sold to Israeli Defence Force / Air Force (IDFAF) arriving in Lydda in April 1952. Allocated the IDFAF serial *20-67*, PT462 served with 105 Sqn. at Ramat David Air Force Base until 1956. It was at this time that all IDFAF Spitfires were replaced by jet aircraft and PT462 was placed into storage.

As part of a programme by the IDFAF, PT462 was one of several Spitfire and Mustang aircraft provided to kibbutz across the country. Kibbutz Kfar-Gaza received PT462 and she remained at the site, eventually being buried on the rubbish dump there due to her deteriorating condition.

The remains of PT462 were recovered by Robert "Robs" Lamplough and returned to the UK in May 1983 before being placed in storage at Fowlmere. Sold to Charles Church and transported to his Micheldever, Hampshire base during July 1984, PT462 was registered G-CTIX.

PT462 in IDFAF service as *20-67*. 22 April 1956. Note clipped wings. *(Image: Zohar Ben Chaim via Peter Arnold Collection)*

Work commenced on the rebuild of PT462 at Micheldever to Spitfire Trainer configuration incorporating the 'Grace-Melton' canopy arrangement *(see ML407)*. The rebuild featured the rebuilt wings along with the Rolls Royce Merlin 66 engine from Spitfire TE517, another Mk.IX also recovered from Israel.

PT462 at Kibbutz Kfar-Gaza in Israel, circa 1970. Note faded *'KJ'* squadron codes from her 4 Sqn. SAAF days. *(Image: Peter Arnold collection)*

PT462 undergoing engines runs shortly after her first flight, Micheldever, 1 August 1987. *(Image: Peter Arnold)*

During the rebuild her wings were modified to incorporate short-span ailerons (Mod 42), as fitted to the Mk.VIII and Mk.XIV, in place of the full-span version fitted to the Mk.IX. This modification remains on the aircraft to this day.

PT462 flew for the first time following the completion of her rebuild on 25 July 1987 with John Lewis at the controls.

PT462 outside the *Charles Church* hangar in *'corporate camouflage'* colours, Micheldever, 20 April 1988. *(Image: Peter Arnold)*

PT462 taking off during *'The Gathering of Spitfires'* at Carefree airport, Arizona on 20 October 1995. *(Image: Peter Arnold)*

Following the tragic death of owner Charles Church on 1 July 1989 whilst flying Spitfire Mk.V EE606, PT462 was sold to Mike Araldi/Jet Cap Aviation and shipped to Bartow, Florida in 1994.

She was registered N462JC in July 1994. It was at this time that PT462 received a new colour scheme to represent her service with 253 Sqn. with codes *SW-A*.

PT462 was sold once again, this time to Anthony Hodgson in February 1998 and regained the registration G-CTIX. She made her way back across the Atlantic to her new home at a private airstrip in Abergale, north Wales and was operated for many years, appearing at numerous airshows and events.

PT462 on the grass at Duxford Airfield, September 2006. *(Image: Jean-Pierre Touzeau)*

PT462 at the hold, waiting for ML407 to land, Duxford Airfield, 10 July 2019. *(Image: Peter Green)*

Acquired by the *Aircraft Restoration Company* in October 2017, PT462 received a more accurate 253 Sqn. colour scheme, retaining the codes *SW-A*. Unfortunately, she suffered a minor 'wheels-up' landing incident at Denham Aerodrome on 27 February 2019 but was quickly returned to airworthy condition.

Operated under the *Aerial Collective* banner with fellow Spitfire Trainer PV202, PT462 is based at Duxford Airfield and provides customer experience flights.

PT462 at rest before the Battle of Britain Airshow, Duxford Airfield on 22 September 2018. *(Image: Peter Arnold)*

MH367 flying over the Hauraki Gulf, near Auckland, soon after her arrival in New Zealand. Owner Doug Brooker flying with Keith Skilling in the rear seat on 22 May 2008. *(Image: Gavin Conroy)*

MH367

Built at Castle Bromwich, MH367 was delivered to 65 Sqn., Kingsnorth, Kent, an Advanced Landing Ground, on 7 August 1943, coded *YT-C*. She was subsequently assigned to 229 Sqn. at RAF Coltishall on 3 September 1944 and served with the squadron until their Mk.IX aircraft were replaced with newer Mk.XVIs, at which point, on 2 December 1944, MH367 was allocated to 312 (Czech) Sqn. at Bradwell Bay, Essex.

After the war, MH367 was issued to the Empire Central Flying School, Hullavington on 11 April 1947. Following an incident in July 1948 with an undercarriage collapse, MH367 was struck off charge and subsequently scrapped.

During 2000, the remains of MH367 were rediscovered in the Flowers scrapyard, near Chippenham, not that far from her old base at RAF Hullavington.

Around the same time, Peter Godfrey, an Englishman living in Florida, was searching for a two-seat Spitfire to

purchase. Harry Stenger, a Florida-based aircraft engineer, heard that Peter Godfrey was looking for a suitable aircraft and approached him with a proposal, which Peter duly accepted. Harry Stenger offered Peter Godfrey one of the Spitfire projects he had recently taken delivery of, a new-build two-seat fuselage manufactured by Dick Melton in the UK (identified as *'DM008'*, i.e. the 8th Spitfire built by Dick Melton).

Peter Godfrey wanted his two-seat Spitfire to have an RAF identity and so the remains of MH367 were incorporated into the project. In addition, the wings and tail from Mk.IX BR601, and the two-seat structure taken out of Mk.IX ML417 *(see ML417)* when she was returned to single-seat configuration were also included in the rebuild.

Interesting image showing the carry-through spar cover from MH367's firewall as recovered from Flowers scrapyard. Note the faded yellow RAF serial *'MH367'* just discernible in the top-left corner. *(Image: Roget Barrett)*

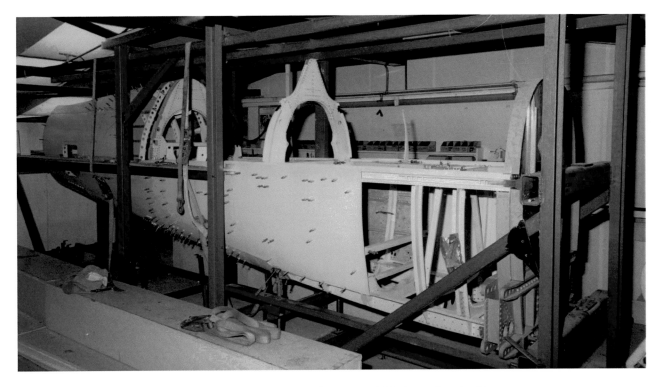

The fuselage of *'DM008'* under construction at Micheldever, Hampshire. 2 May 1991. *(Image: Peter Arnold)*

MH367 under restoration in Harry Stenger's workshop at Bartow Executive Airport, Florida on 22 December 2004. *(Image: John Sanderson)*

Her rebuild complete, MH367's first post-restoration flight was in November 2006. She emerged wearing the striking markings of *Mk.V ER570/WD-Q*, the personal aircraft of Major Robert Levine, 4 Fighter Squadron, 52 Fighter Group USAAF, when based in Tunisia, North Africa during June 1943.

MH367 was subsequently purchased by New Zealander Doug Brooker in December 2007 and shipped to Auckland, where she arrived in spring 2008.

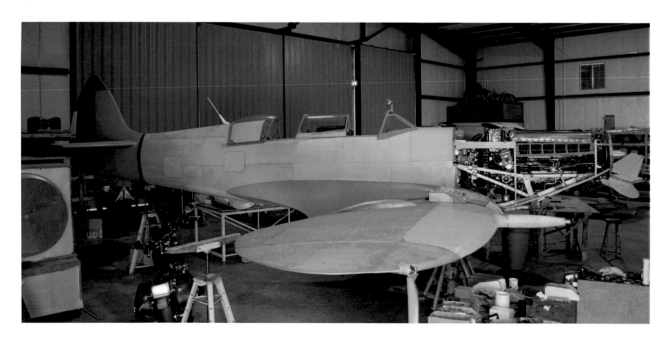

Another image of MH367 under restoration at Bartow, circa early 2005. *(Image: Harry Stenger via Peter Arnold collection)*

Owner Peter Godfrey in the rear seat taking his first flight in MH367 during November 2006. *(Image: Harry Stenger via Peter Arnold collection)*

She was repainted to represent *Mk.IX EN520/FL-A*, the personal aircraft of Wg. Cdr. Colin F. Gray DSO DFC and two bars. Wg. Cdr. Gray was New Zealand's top-scoring fighter ace during the Second World War when he commanded 81 Sqn., in Algeria, 1943. He finished the war with 27½ confirmed kills.

MH367 is based at Ardmore Airport, Auckland, New Zealand as part of the NZ Warbirds Association where she is operated by *Warbirds Adventure Rides* providing customer experience flights.

Liz Needham flying MH367, with Frank Parker in Mk.XIV NH799, near Ardmore, New Zealand in June 2015. *(Image: Nicholas McIndoe)*

MH367 and friend on a photoshoot near Ardmore, New Zealand, 5 December 2012. Owner Doug Brooker flying with Dave Brown in the rear seat. (*Image: Gavin Conroy*)

SM520 over the Oxfordshire countryside, at the launch of the *Boultbee Flight Academy* in July 2011. Former *Battle of Britain Memorial Flight* C/O Sqn. Ldr. Al Pinner MBE flying with Battle of Britain pilot Wg. Cdr. *'Tim'* Elkington in the rear seat. *(Image: Richard Paver)*

SM520

SM520 was built at Castle Bromwich as an HF Mk.IXe fitted with a Merlin 70 powerplant. She was taken on charge by the RAF at 33 MU, RAF Lyneham on 23 November 1944.

SM520 did not see RAF squadron service and spent time in storage at several Maintenance Units before being purchased as part of the one hundred and thirty-six (136) Spitfire aircraft ordered by the South African Air Force (SAAF) in March 1946. Dispatched to 47 MU at RAF Sealand for packing, SM520 was placed onboard the ship *Halesius* from Birkenhead Docks, Liverpool on 27 May 1948, arriving in Durban, South Africa on 21 June.

The serial allocated to SM520 in South African Air Force service is believed to be *SAAF 5572*, but this is not confirmed. Therefore, details of SM520's service within the SAAF are limited. The Spitfires in the SAAF initially served in the frontline fighter role, but they also carried out other duties, including a Central Flying School assignment to train pilots destined to fly the SAAF P-51 Mustang in the Korean War during the early 1950s.

Following her SAAF service, SM520 was struck off charge and sold for scrap in 1954. The South African Air Force Museum secured her remains which were stored along with many other Spitfire wrecks in a compound at Snake Valley, arriving in November 1977.

The remains of SM520 were traded to Steve W. Atkins and shipped to the UK in 1989. Passing the project on to Alan Dunkerley, a new single-seat fuselage, incorporating the many usable components from SM520, was built by Tony Choong near Oxford. The fuselage was complete by 1995.

Registered as G-BXHZ in June 1997, no further work was undertaken until she was offered for sale and purchased by Paul Portelli in June 2002. She was re-registered as G-ILDA on 11 July 2002.

SM520 single-seat fuselage in storage, Edenfield, Lancashire, 26 April 2002. (Image: Stephen Huckvale via Peter Arnold Collection)

It was at this time that a decision was made to convert SM520 to two-seat configuration and the fuselage was shipped to *Airframe Assemblies* who undertook the work. The fuselage, now in two-seat Spitfire Trainer configuration, was transported to Thruxton in April 2004 for completion of the project to airworthy condition.

Paul Portelli died on 20 May 2007, meaning he sadly never saw his Spitfire fly. SM520 flew once again on 17 October 2008 from Thruxton, painted in a stunning RNethAF scheme to represent BS147 as *H-99* (*see BS147*). She was subsequently put up for sale, this time at an auction held by Bonhams in London on 20 April 2009. The successful bidder was Steve Boultbee Brooks.

SM520 now converted to two-seat Trainer configuration, under restoration at Thruxton. 20 May 2004. *(Image: Peter Arnold)*

'Double-Dutch' !! PV202 and SM520 in spurious RNethAF markings as 'H-98' and 'H-99' respectively, at Duxford Airfield on 20 March 2009. *(Image: Bob Southall / Peter Arnold collection)*

During her period of flight testing, this is a further shot of SM520 in RNethAF markings. She is being flown by Johnathan Whalley, who is accompanied by his wife in the rear seat. March 2009. *(Image: Richard Paver)*

SOLD!!! The moment the hammer went down at Bonhams, 20 April 2009. Note the Richard Paver shot of SM520 in RNethAF markings being used during the auction. *(Image: Peter Arnold)*

Pilot Al Pinner, former C/O of the *Battle of Britain Memorial Flight*, with famous wartime fighter pilot Geoffrey Wellum DFC in the rear seat of SM520, at the launch of the *Boultbee Flight Academy* held at Oxford Airport in July 2011. Geoffrey Wellum was heard saying to Al Pinner before they got out, "That was fine, I can clear you to go solo". *(Image: Richard Paver)*

A wonderful study of SM520 wearing invasion stripes, on 3 June 2019, to commemorate the 74th anniversary of the D-Day landings. Note these markings were worn for a few weeks only. *(Image: Darren Harbar via Matt Jones)*

She was repainted and emerged in a late-war European theatre camouflage scheme, wearing the squadron codes *KJ-I* as a reference to the former 4 Sqn. SAAF Mk.V Spitfire which was converted to two-seat configuration in 1944 *(see ES127)*, as well as providing a visible connection back to SM520's SAAF heritage.

SM520 is operated by the *Boultbee Flight Academy*, the world's only Spitfire training school, offering passenger experience flights from Goodwood Aerodrome, Lee-on-Solent Airport & Exeter Airport.

SM520 taking off from Lee-On-Solent Airfield on 6 June 2019. *(Image: Mark Rutley Photography)*

Matt Jones sitting on the wing of SM520 on 7 May 2020. Note the *'Thank You NHS'* heart, one of three applied to SM520 in appreciation of the amazing work performed by the UK National Health Service during the Covid-19 crisis. *(Image: Matt Jones/Boultbee Flight Academy)*

SM520 being flown by Matt Jones on 8 May 2020 during a special flypast across the south of England to commemorate the 75th anniversary of VE-Day and to honour several veterans and care providers. *(Image: Malcolm R Wells - Chief Photographer - The News Portsmouth 1990-2015)*

SM520 breaking away from the camera-ship during a photo sortie in 2010. (*Image: Richard Paver*)

NH341 being flown by Flt. Lt. 'Parky' Parkinson over the Kent coast on her public debut in April 2017. *(Image: Richard Paver)*

NH341

NH341 was built at Castle Bromwich as a low-level fighter (LF Mk.IXe) and delivered to No.8 Maintenance Unit on 28 April 1944. She was sent to Miles Aircraft for modifications before delivery to the only squadron she served with, 411 (Grizzly Bear) Squadron, Royal Canadian Air Force (RCAF) on 12 June 1944. NH341 undertook twenty-seven operational sorties over France in the hands of nine Canadian pilots.

One of her pilots, Lt. Col. (RCAF) T.R. *Tommy* Wheler MBE DFC CD Legion d'Honneur, travelled from his Canadian home during 2015 to be reunited with NH341 one more time. *Tommy* sadly died in October 2018 at the grand age of 97.

NH341's colour scheme faithfully replicates the time she was being flown by F/O A.B. *Bruce* Whiteford when he had his wife's name *'Elizabeth'* and her initials *'EO'* painted on the aircraft. F/O Whiteford's first mission on 14 June 1944 *(Ramrod No.1000)* was to provide high level escort for 200+ Avro Lancaster bombers on a raid to target the E-boat base at Le Havre, France.

Flt. Lt. H.C. *Charlie* Trainor secured his third kill in 48 hours whilst flying NH341 on 29 June 1944 when he

downed a Bf109 five miles west of Caen. He went on to destroy another Bf109 on the evening of 30 June 1944 over Thury-Harcourt, again flying NH341. Flt. Lt. Trainor went on to gain Ace status and was awarded the DSO and DFC.

On 2 July 1944, W/O J.S. *Jimmy* Jeffrey was flying a morning patrol in NH341 when he was engaged by Fw190s south-east of Caen and shot down. W/O Jeffrey bailed out, successfully evaded capture and was back in the UK by late August.

The wreckage of NH341 was recovered during the early 1990s and incorporated, along with other Spitfire wrecks, into a diorama display within the *Musée Mémorial Bataille de Normandie* at Bayeux in France.

The wreckage of NH341 was subsequently acquired by *Aero Legends*, who commissioned *Airframe Assemblies Ltd* to commence the initial build of the fuselage. The fuselage was passed to *Historic Flying Ltd* at Duxford Airfield on 23 July 2015 to continue this build and to complete the work to airworthy condition.

Composite diorama made up from several Spitfires, including NH341 and ML295, on display at the *Musée Mémorial Bataille de Normandie*, Bayeux, France during September 2002. *(Image: Jean-Pierre Touzeau)*

Former pilot, Tommy Wheler, during his 2015 visit to see the rebuild of NH341 in the *Historic Flying Ltd.* workshop at Duxford Airfield. *(Image: Ady Shaw)*

NH341 under rebuild in the *Historic Flying Ltd.* hangar at Duxford Airfield during 2016. *(Image: Greg Davis)*

In the later part of 2015, during a visit to the workshop from his home in Canada, former pilot *Tommy* Wheler signed an access panel on NH341 and viewed progress of her rebuild.

Upon completion, NH341 took to the skies on her first post-restoration flight from Duxford Airfield on 11 March 2017.

NH341 over the Kent coast, April 2017. *(Image: Richard Paver)*

Sundown at Headcorn. NH341, along with single-seat stablemate TD314, at rest, 2 June 2018. *(Image: Jason Elmore)*

NH341, or *'Elizabeth'* as she is now fondly known, carries out customer experience flights from both the *Aero Legends* base at Headcorn, Kent, as well as North Weald, Essex which was famously important during The Battle of Britain.

NH341 in front of the WWI-era Belfast-Truss hangars at Duxford Airfield on 5 April 2019. *(Image: Peter Green)*

Flt. Lt. *Parky* Parkinson flying NH341, along with PV202 flown by Flt. Lt. Charlie Brown on a joint sortie out of Headcorn Aerodrome, Kent during 2018. *(Image: Richard Paver)*

UNDERGOING REBUILD

Due to the huge popularity of people wanting to take to the skies in a Spitfire, there are a growing number of two-seat restoration projects being undertaken to pristine, airworthy condition.

This chapter provides the histories of the aircraft that are currently under restoration along with those that are planned.

There are however, two Spitfire Trainer projects underway that have yet to officially release their RAF serial identity and they are therefore not detailed within the book.

RAF Serial	Civil Reg	Notes
BS410	G-TCHI	Under rebuild, Pent Farm, Kent
EN570	LN-AOA	Under rebuild, Sandown, Isle of Wight
BS548	--	Under rebuild, Sandown, Isle of Wight
Serial withheld #1	--	Under rebuild, Biggin Hill, Kent
Serial withheld #2	--	Location withheld
EN179	G-TCHO	Project

Spitfire Mk.IX Trainer BS410 shown here in the *Vintage Aero* hangar at Pent Farm near Hythe, Kent in early 2020. *(Image: Flypast – Jamie Ewan)*

BS410

Built at Chattis Hill dispersal factory in Hampshire, BS410 first flew on 28 October 1942 before being taken on charge by the RAF and allocated to 315 (City of Dęblin) Sqn. at Northolt on 6 November (just one day before EN179 arrived at the same squadron, see *EN179*). Initially BS410 received the squadron codes *PK-E* but later changed to *PK-A* during April 1943.

BS410 was dispatched to Air Service Training at Hamble for modifications on 15 March 1943 before returning to 315 Sqn. at Northolt.

BS410 was flown by several squadron pilots, including Capt. Francis *'Gabby'* Gabreski, a Polish-American who went on to become the USAAF's top-scoring pilot in the European Theatre with 34½ confirmed kills.

On 13 May 1943, with pilot F/O Piotr Kuryllowicz at the controls, BS410 was escorting USAAF B-17s on a bombing mission to the Potez aircraft factory. The formation was attacked by large numbers of Bf109s and Fw190s resulting in several aircraft being shot down,

including BS410. F/O Kuryllowicz bailed out and escaped by parachute, landing safely on the ground. He was soon captured and spent the remainder of the war in a PoW camp. BS410 crashed into marshland near Occoches, north of Amiens, France.

Above: The accurately recreated 315 Sqn. emblem on BS410's rebuilt fuselage. *(Image: John Sanderson)*

Capt. *'Gabby'* Gabreski in BS410/*PK-E* during early 1943. *(Image: Peter Arnold collection)*

The wreckage of BS410 was recovered from the marsh by members of *The Association of Somme Aviation 39-45* in December 2005. Acquired by Martin Phillips during 2007, the remains of BS410 were transported to the UK and placed in storage.

BS410 was registered on 19 November 2009 as G-TCHI. During May 2009, her former wartime pilot Piotr Kuryllowicz visited the rebuild of BS410 at *Airframe Assemblies Ltd.*, on the Isle of Wight, where he was able to sit in her cockpit once again.

BS410 wearing authentic 315 Sqn. colours, shown here at Biggin Hill on 16 July 2016. *(Image: John Sanderson)*

BS410 was transported to the *Biggin Hill Heritage Hangar*, arriving on 26 January 2016, where she underwent restoration work and received an authentic 315 (Dęblin) Sqn. colour scheme to reflect the markings she wore whilst serving with the squadron. BS410 recently moved to the *Vintage Aero* facility at Pent Farm, Kent where restoration continues with a target to have her flying in 2021.

BS410 in the Vintage Aero hangar at Pent Farm near Hythe in Kent during early 2020. *(Image: Flypast – Jamie Ewan)*

EN570

Although initially ordered as a Mk.V, EN570 flew for the first time as a Mk.IX on 3 April 1943 following conversion by Rolls Royce at Hucknall. Accepted by the RAF, EN570 was dispatched to 15 MU at Wroughton on 8 April 1943, then to 76 MU at the same site on 21 April.

Allocated to 611 (West Lancashire) Sqn. at Biggin Hill as *FY-J*, EN570 arrived on 15 May 1943. During her short time at the squadron EN570 scored two kills whilst being flown by pilot Flt. Lt. V.A. Lancaster. Flt. Lt. Lancaster's first kill was a Bf109 on 17 May 1943 and his second a Fw190 on 30 May.

Taking part in Rodeo 229, a mission to perform fighter sweeps over the Pas-de-Calais area of northern France on 11 June 1943, EN570 was one of twenty-four (24) Spitfires from both 611 and 341 Squadrons who encountered thirteen (13) Fw190 aircraft from JG26/Gruppe II.

Unfortunately, EN570 became the only casualty of the encounter, when Obfw. Adolf Glunz shot her down near Saint-Pol-sur-Ternoise, north-east of Abbeville to become his thirty-third (33) victory.

EN570 and her pilot, F/O Gordon Rowland Lindsay, were sadly lost. EN570 impacted the ground in a woodland near the town of Lucheux, northern France. F/O Lindsay's body was later recovered and is today buried within the Saint Pierre cemetery in Amiens. He was just 24.

The wreckage of EN570 was recovered on 10 July 2013 by members by *The Association of Somme Aviation 39-45*. She was acquired by the *Norwegian Flying Aces* organisation, and a programme commenced to return her to airworthy condition once more.

Recovered Rolls Royce Merlin engine from EN570 on display within the house of Pierre Ben (the President of Somme Aviation) in the town of Warloy-Baillon, near Amiens, France. 6 August 2017. *(Image: Jean-Pierre Touzeau)*

EN570 in the jig at Airframe Assemblies, Isle of Wight, during May 2018. *(Image: Runar Vassbotten / Norwegian Flying Aces)*

EN570's starboard wing out of the jig at Biggin Hill, 11 June 2019. *(Image: John Sanderson)*

The fuselage of EN570 out of the jig at *Airframe Assemblies*, Isle of Wight, 10 December 2019. *(Image: Peter Arnold)*

The decision was made to rebuild the aircraft in two-seat Trainer configuration, incorporating the lower profile 'Grace-Melton' style canopy. A fuselage was built at *Airframe Assemblies Ltd.* on the Isle of Wight, and a set of wings have been built at the *Biggin Hill Heritage Hangar*.

As announced by the *Norwegian Flying Aces* in early April 2020, EN570 will emerge from rebuild wearing the codes *FY-J* of 611 Sqn. These colours and markings commemorate both her time with the unit during 1943 at Biggin Hill, and Norwegian pilot Lt. Rolf Thorbjørn Tradin who flew EN570 . Lt. Tradin secured Norway's first air victory whilst flying a Gloster Gladiator on 9 April 1940, when he downed a Me110 during the Nazi invasion of Norway.

Once complete, the intention is to operate EN570 in Norway for passenger experience flights.

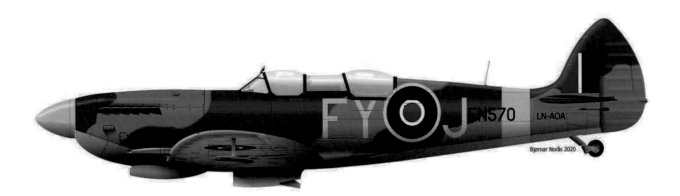

EN570 wearing the markings she will emerge in once complete. *(Image: Bjørnar Norås via Norwegian Flying Aces)*

An image taken from wartime footage showing BS548 when she served with 340 (Alsace) Sqn. during 1942. *(Image: Peter Arnold collection)*

BS548

Originally ordered as a Mk.V, BS548 was completed as a Mk.IX by Rolls Royce at Hucknall and took her first flight on 31 October 1942. She was taken on charge by the RAF, allocated to 340 (Île-de-France) Sqn. at Biggin Hill on 7 November 1942 and given the codes *GW-B*.

Dispatched to Air Service Training at Hamble for modifications on 10 December 1942, BS548 was subsequently allocated to 402 (City of Winnipeg) Sqn. RCAF at Kenley on 31 January 1943. Whilst on a Ramrod mission to Rouen, BS548 suffered Cat.Ac damage (beyond the unit's capability to repair) from a Fw190 on 12 March 1943. With the repairs completed at base, BS548 transferred back to Biggin Hill, this time to 341 (Alsace) Sqn. on 2 April 1943.

During a Circus mission (daytime bomber attack with fighter escort) over northern France on 17 April 1943, with pilot Lt. Claude Raoul-Duval at the controls, BS548 was shot down near Tancarville, 20-miles east of Le Havre in Normandy, by a Fw190 flown by Fw. Herbert Gumprecht of 11/JG2.

Lt. Raoul-Duval survived the crash, and managing to avoid capture, returned to 341 Sqn. in the UK via Spain and Gibraltar six months later.

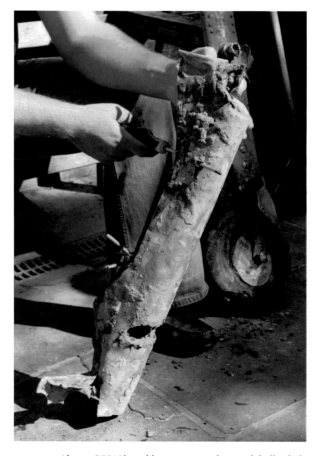

Above: BS548's rudder post, complete with bullet-hole highlighted here by a screwdriver. *(Image: Jeff Carless)*

Left: BS548's former pilot, Claude Raoul-Duval, flanked by dig team members Steve Vizard (left) and Gareth Jones (right). They are showing him the rear view mirror just recovered from the excavation, to which he quickly responded "I wish I'd looked in the bloody thing..." *(Image: 'The French Connection')*

The exact location of BS548's crash-site was identified by local researcher Laurent Viton, in marshland near Tancarville. A recovery operation was undertaken during September 2012, with pilot Claude Raoul-Duval present to see the wreckage of his former aircraft emerge.

The remains were acquired by Australian Ross Pay, and *Airframe Assemblies Ltd.* were commissioned to build the fuselage, which is well underway at their Isle of Wight facility.

It has been revealed that BS548 will emerge in the fullness of time from her rebuild with the 'Grace-Melton' style canopy configuration.

Above: The recovered rear-view mirror from BS548, signed by pilot Claude Raoul-Duval. *(Image: Steve Vizard)*

Left: BS548 under rebuild at *Airframe Assemblies Ltd*, Isle of Wight, 1 June 2020. *(Image: Chris Michell)*

Awaiting the next scramble. EN179/SZ-J *'Jasia'* at RAF Northolt with 316 Sqn. during the summer of 1943. (*Image: Wojtek Matusiak collection via Peter Arnold*)

EN179

Built at Eastleigh as a single-seat Spitfire Mk.IX, EN179 flew for the first time on 31 October 1942. Accepted by the RAF, EN179 was allocated to 315 (City of Dęblin) Sqn. at Northolt on 7 November 1942 and given the codes *PK-X*. She was dispatched to Air Service Training at Hamble for modifications on 21 January 1943 before returning to Northolt and joining the Station Flight as *RF-K* on 29 January.

Assigned to 306 (City of Toruń) Sqn., also at Northolt, on 23 February 1943, EN179 was allocated the codes *UZ-J*. Within weeks, on 14 March 1943, EN179 had moved to another Polish squadron, this time to 316 (City of Warsaw) Sqn. and still at Northolt. She initially retained the individual letter 'J' just adopting her new squadron's codes, becoming *SZ-J* (with the name *'Jasia'*), but later changed to *SZ-C*.

EN179 is credited with destroying a Fw190 on 9 July 1943 whilst on a Ramrod mission being flown by pilot Sgt. A. Murkowski. During a Ramrod mission (bomber attack against ground targets) over Northern France on 19 August 1943, EN179 was engaged by Fw190s and shot down, with the sad loss of pilot F/O Andrzej Feliks Michal Próchnicki. EN179 crashed close to the village of Naours, near Amiens, France.

F/O Próchnicki was initially buried in Naours cemetery, before being moved to the Polish Cemetery in Grainville-Langannerie. He was 26.

The buried wreckage of EN179 was recovered by *The Association of Somme Aviation 39-45* in August 2005. Subsequently acquired by Martin Phillips during 2008, EN179 was registered G-TCHO on 12 December of the same year. The remains of EN179 were transported to the UK and placed in storage.

It was announced by *Aero Legends* in February 2020 that EN179 will be rebuilt as a two-seat aircraft. No further details or timeline for completion has been offered at this time.

HOW CAN I FLY IN A SPITFIRE?

The obvious questions are: "Can I fly in a Spitfire?"; "Where can I do it?" and "How much will it cost?". Well, up until a few years ago the answer to the first question was essentially 'No', that was unless you knew one of the aircraft owners and were either gifted a flight (sometimes offered to veterans or royalty) or you 'shared the cost' of a flight. However, in the middle of 2014 the CAA relaxed their stance and introduced CAP 1395 Safety Standards Acknowledgement and Consent (SSAC). Flights in a Spitfire are covered within the rules for 'Class 2: Experience flight in a Historic (single engine piston) warbird'.

Essentially, the rules outline the framework under which such flights can be safely offered to the public. The CAA wants the potential passenger to understand that an 80-year-old, former single-seat fighter, is not and was never intended to have the safety features of a modern Airbus. In addition, the document states that 'Applicants should consider all potential hazards. Potential hazards are likely to include, but are not restricted to, engine failure, engine fire, component failure, mid-air collision, heavy landing, fuel exhaustion, pilot incapacitation, ditching and adverse weather'. Spitfire flight operators are obliged to provide suitable training for all participants which outlines the risks involved, and the procedures to follow, in the event of an emergency. This training is delivered via either a training video or one-to-one demonstration.

Other considerations include: Type of airfield - grass or tarmac runway? Air Traffic Control (ATC) - small airfield with one controller or full ATC function? Fire Station - a bucket of water or fire engines? Who will your pilot be? You get the idea - think carefully about what you are doing!

So, you have considered the risks and you still want to proceed, so who can you fly with and which aircraft can you fly?

The increase in the number of airworthy two-seat Spitfires has provided more choice than ever before. At the time of writing there are **NINE** airworthy aircraft available to take a flight in, namely the unique prototype Mk.VIII MT818, along with Mk.IX's MH367, MJ627, MJ772, ML407, NH341, PT462, PV202, & SM520.

At the time of writing the restoration of Mk.IX TE308 at Biggin Hill is almost complete and will become airworthy in the near future. It may be, that by the time you read this book, there are TEN airworthy Spitfires Trainers.

Left: Co-author Greg Davis in the rear cockpit of PV202 over the Kent countryside on 17 July 2018. *(Image: Greg Davis)*

BEFORE YOU FLY – IMPORTANT INFORMATION

1. Most operators will let you take control of the Spitfire, at the pilot's discretion of course.

2. Make sure you read the operating company's insurance terms and conditions carefully to make sure you know the level of cover you are getting.

3. Lots of companies advertise Spitfire flights, but many are merely brokers for the operators already mentioned. Be cautious, some adverts state they can get you a flight in aircraft overseas. Before you book it is worth checking the last known condition of the aircraft, as there are adverts for flights in aircraft that have not flown for some considerable time.

4. All Spitfire experience flights in the UK are regulated by the CAA and high standards of protective equipment are mandatory for all operators. This may not be the case in other countries.

A flight in a two-seat Spitfire will therefore cost anywhere between £1,930 *approx.* ($4,050 NZD) for a 25-minute flight through to £12,000 for a dogfight with a Bf109 over the English Channel. Always check the Terms and Conditions carefully, in addition to your life and critical illness cover. Ensure that you meet the size and weight criteria for your chosen aircraft. The maximum height is 6'6" (198cm) and the maximum weight is 16st 7lb (105kg). In addition to weight, shape and flexibility is important. The rear control stick must have full movement and so a large waistline may preclude you from flying. Check with your doctor that you are healthy enough to undergo what is euphemistically called a 'Dynamic Experience'!

Go on, give us a wave! NH341 getting airborne from Headcorn, Kent on 29 June 2019, with passenger Mike Wormington from Virginia, USA, who travelled over especially for his flight experience. *(Image: Roger Barrett)*

IS FLYING IN A SPITFIRE EXPENSIVE?

The cost of flying in a Spitfire is not an insignificant amount of money for most people. However, you can consider it in one of two ways. The first is that you are getting a 'once in a lifetime' Spitfire flight experience which for many is more than enough! The second is to understand how much it costs to acquire and then operate an airworthy Spitfire.

So how do you begin? You will first need to acquire a two-seat Spitfire along with a spare overhauled Merlin engine. This along with an appropriate spare-parts holding is going to cost you in the region of £4,000,000.

Then, you need to determine how often you are going to fly her. Let us assume that your Spitfire is going to fly 500 hours per year, this then reflects the overhaul cycle for a Merlin engine. The engine overhaul needs to be carried out by a CAA authorised organisation.

We provide some broad estimates here to give an insight into the costs involved in owning and operating a two-seat Spitfire. Please keep in mind that these are indicative costs only.

The breakdown below is overly simplistic, but it highlights the large costs involved. Operating a Spitfire is not an easy or cheap business to be in but mixed into all these operations is a real passion to share these amazing aircraft and highlight their incredibly important chapter in our world history.

Annual costs to operate a two-seat Spitfire, based on 500 flying hours per annuum, would be in the region of the following,

Expense	Cost
Merlin engine overhaul	£200,000
Prop overhaul	£80,000
Insurance	£70,000
Routine maintenance*	£35,000
Fuel	£250,000
Pilot/staffing costs	£220,000
Hangar & airfield costs	£75,000
Spares (as needed)	£30,000
Marketing & advertising	£50,000
Total (per annum)**	**£1,010,000**

Inspections every 25 flying hours, getting progressively more detailed on each inspection up to 100-hour check, they then revert back to the 25-hour check and begin the cycle once again. In addition, engine-cam inspections are required every 25 hours, and undercarriage checks are conducted every 150 landings for some components and 300 landings for others.

**These costs assume no unforeseen issues*

Freshly overhauled Rolls Royce Merlin engine arrives at Biggin Hill, 22 November 2019. *(Image: Greg Davis)*

And this is what a Merlin looks like when installed in an aircraft, in this case TE308. It takes many hours for engineers to get from the top image to this one. Taken at Biggin Hill on 10 March 2020. *(Image: Roger Barrett)*

WHO OFFERS SPITFIRE FLIGHTS?

There are several operators offering Spitfire experience flights. In this chapter we provide a breakdown for each of them along with the various experiences they provide.

Important Notes

1. Information provided within this chapter is for guidance only.

2. Spitfire flight operators may change, withdraw, or add available aircraft and/or experiences depending upon serviceability. All interested parties should contact the Spitfire operators directly for up-to-date pricing and available experiences/aircraft.

3. The authors make no recommendation and instruct any prospective passenger to conduct their own due diligence prior to entering into any financial transaction relating to experience flights.

4. Information provided in this chapter is correct at time of publication (July 2020).

Aerial Collective

Aircraft Operated	Spitfire Mk.IX Trainer PT462 Spitfire Mk.IX Trainer PV202
Location	Duxford Airfield, Cambridgeshire
Flight Experiences Offered	Fly in a Spitfire
Flight Durations Offered	30/50 minutes
Cost	From £2,750
Included	Logbook (signed by pilot) & flight patch Entry to IWM Duxford museum (x2 people)
Add-ons	Video of your Spitfire flight available to purchase
Website	www.aerialcollective.co.uk

Below: *Aerial Collective's two-seater Spitfire duo (PV202 and PT462) captured here towards the end of a chilly October 2018 day at Duxford Airfield. (Image: Peter Green)*

Aero Legends

Aircraft Operated	Spitfire Mk.IX Trainer NH341 *'Elizabeth'* Spitfire Mk.IX Trainer PV202 *(as required)*
Location	Headcorn Aerodrome, Kent North Weald Airfield, Essex Sywell Aerodrome, Northamptonshire
Flight Experiences Offered	Fly in a Spitfire Formation Spitfire Flight (2x two-seat Spitfire)
Flight Durations Offered	20/30/40/60 minutes
Cost	From £2,750
Included	Squadron print signed by pilot after your flight
Add-ons	Video of your Spitfire flight available to purchase
Website	www.aerolegends.co.uk

Below: *Aero Legends* NH341 taxiing out at Headcorn Aerodrome, Kent during 2019. *(Image: Stuart Gennery)*

Boultbee Flight Academy

Aircraft Operated	Spitfire Mk.IX Trainer SM520
Location	Goodwood Aerodrome, West Sussex Lee-on-Solent Airport, Hampshire Exeter Airport, Devon *(see website for dates & experiences available at each location)*
Flight Experiences Offered	Fly in a Spitfire Fly in a Spitfire – formation with a Mk.IX Spitfire Formation Spitfire Flight (2x two-seat Spitfire) Fighter appreciation Flight (2x two-seat Spitfire plus Bf109)
Flight Durations Offered	30/45/55 minutes
Cost	From £2,750
Included	-
Add-ons	Video of your Spitfire flight available to purchase
Website	www.boultbeeflightacademy.co.uk/spitfire-flights

Left: Off We Go!! *Boultbee Flight Academy* operated Mk.IX Trainer SM520 undergoing engine power checks before take-off at Duxford Airfield, 9 March 2017. *(Image: Peter Green)*

Classic Wings

Aircraft Operated	Spitfire Mk.IX Trainer PT462 Spitfire Mk.IX Trainer PV202
Location	Duxford Airfield, Cambridgeshire
Flight Experiences Offered	Fly in a Spitfire Fly with a Spitfire (in De Havilland Dragon Rapide)
Flight Durations Offered	30/50 minutes
Cost	From £2,750
Included	Flight certificate Flight suit badge Professional photo in the cockpit Entry to IWM Duxford museum
Add-ons	-
Website	www.classic-wings.co.uk/fly-in-a-spitfire

Left: *Classic Wings* utilise both PV202 and PT462 for their experience flights. They are both shown here flying over Duxford Airfield on 19 September 2019. *(Image: Peter Green)*

Fly a Spitfire (Biggin Hill Heritage Hangar)

Aircraft Operated	Spitfire Mk.VIII Trainer MT818 *(as required)* Spitfire Mk.IX Trainer MJ627 Spitfire Mk.IX Trainer MJ772
Location	Biggin Hill Airport, Kent
Flight Experiences Offered	Fly in a Spitfire Formation Spitfire Flight (2x two-seat Spitfire)
Flight Durations Offered	20/35/45/60 minutes
Cost	From £2,750
Included	Video of your Spitfire flight
Add-ons	Upgrade: Flight-time extension Upgrade: Add a single-seat Spitfire to your two-seat flight and fly in formation Upgrade: Wing-to-wing with GA8 Airvan chase plane
Website	www.flyaspitfire.com

Below: MJ627 pulls alongside the Airvan chase plane over Kent, 31 July 2018. *(Image: Richard Paver)*

Ultimate Warbird Flights

Aircraft Operated	Spitfire Mk.IX Trainer ML407 *'The Grace Spitfire'*
Location	Sywell Aerodrome, Northamptonshire
Flight Experiences Offered	Fly in a Spitfire
Flight Durations Offered	25 minutes
Cost	From £2,790
Included	Welcome pack (Pilots notes, Popup Spitfire card, Flight information card)
Add-ons	Video of your Spitfire flight available to purchase Upgrade: Flight-time extension Upgrade: Wing-to-wing with Blades Aerobatic Display Team's Extra EA-300 aircraft
Website	www.warbirdflights.co.uk/spitfireml407

Left: Carolyn Grace flying ML407 on 9 October 2012. *(Image: Darren Harbar via Ultimate Warbird Flights)*

Warbird Adventure Rides

Aircraft Operated	Spitfire Mk.IX Trainer MH367
Location	Ardmore Airport, Papakura (near Auckland), New Zealand
Flight Experiences Offered	Fly in a Spitfire Formation Flight (Spitfire with P-51 and/or P-40)
Flight Durations Offered	25 minutes
Cost	From $4,050 NZD (£1,930 GBP approx.)
Included	-
Add-ons	Video of your Spitfire flight available to purchase
Website	www.warbird.co.nz

Below: The best seat in the house!! A passenger's view of pilot Liz Needham flying MH367 over Waitawa Regional Park, near Auckland. *(Image: Warbird Adventure Rides)*

WHAT IS IT LIKE TO FLY IN A SPITFIRE?

In this chapter co-author Greg Davis relates the amazing Spitfire Trainer flights he has been fortunate enough to experience over the last few years.

These accounts give the reader a flavour of what it feels like to fly in these incredible aircraft and also provides an insight into both the humbling and adrenaline-inducing effect they have on the passenger.

These accounts were previously posted to *The Two-Seat Spitfire Page* on Facebook.

Flight No.1: MJ627

(30 March 2016)

Please do not read this if you are in a hurry or do not have the time! Make yourself a coffee, sit down and hopefully you will enjoy this account of one of the most exciting days of my life!

I had previously been frustrated when my Spitfire flight was cancelled. However, yesterday I was at work, minding my own business, when I received an email from Biggin Hill Heritage Hangar. It said, "We have had a cancellation for a flight in MJ627 and wondered if you could get here in time to utilise it". Scramble!!

I dropped everything and set off for Biggin Hill. When I arrived, we dealt with the financial vulgarities and I was then ushered into the briefing room, where I watched two excellently produced safety presentations. The first one covered why the CAA can now authorise flights in the Spitfire and the nature of the risks involved. The second video covered emergency procedures such as how to get out of the aircraft, how to use the parachute and the nature of the safety equipment provided. Both these presentations were highly reassuring and informative. Having watched the presentations and having had an opportunity to ask questions, I was then required to sign consent forms, accepting the terms and conditions of my flight.

I should add at this point, that I had already had sight of the agreement form and it had suggested that I contact my life insurance and critical illness insurance companies in order to understand what effect my flight might have on my cover. In my case, the life insurance companies were fine but the critical illness companies would not cover my flight should I be critically injured.

Next, I was led to the kit room, to collect my protective gear and helmet. The previous passenger flight was just returning, meaning it would soon be my turn.

I was ushered out onto the apron outside the hangar and met my fantastic pilot for the day, Don Sigourney. Don was an absolute gentleman and took time to work out what I did and did not want to do, and we agreed a route that took in a fly past over my house!

The ever present and helpful James helped me into the aircraft and attached me to the parachute. They say that you do not get in a Spitfire, you put it on. I now know what they mean! It is a cosy place to be. While James is sorting my GoPro and intercom, Don was outside checking the plane, as he does before every flight. Very reassuring.

Don is now ready for the off and seeks permission from the control tower. We then start the Merlin and begin our taxi. At a prearranged spot Don stops, turns the Spit into the wind and does a full power test - best check that all 1750hp is present and correct before we take off!

Circling Biggin Hill in MJ627. *(Image: Greg Davis)*

We then move to the end of the runway and in a few seconds, and a few feet, we are airborne. We are heading west but our route takes us east, so Don gives it 1700 rpm and boost 6. We soar into a sweeping right-hand arc that points us eastwards. Don backs off the power and we reach level flight at 1800 feet...just seconds ago we were at zero feet and heading west.

Don points out the landmarks, Biggin Hill and Westerham on the right and the Shard and the City of London a mere 7 miles away on our left. He then asks me if I would like to take control! I cannot really explain what it feels like to be offered control of a multi-million-pound Spitfire with 1750hp. It is simultaneously exhilarating and slightly overwhelming. Having explained to me what we were going to do, and how sensitive the Spitfire is to the control of the stick, Don says those unbelievable words, "You have control!" Gulp.

I take control of the Spitfire and endeavour to maintain a level flight path. A movement of the stick backwards sends us rising from the straight and level and an equally small movement forwards sends us into a downward path. I very quickly realised that the movement of a few

millimetres moves the Spitfire instantly. I dread to think what a sudden violent movement to the left would do! I persist in trying to make small movements.

At 200 mph we are nipping across Kent very quickly and I give control back to the expert hands of Don, who makes level flight seem easy! Don has studied his map and is tracking over the green fields of Kent towards my house. Unbeknown to me, my son has tracked us online and my wife is in our front garden to see my Spitfire fly over our house at 1800ft and 211mph! We then need to make a huge turn in order to head back in the direction of Biggin Hill. I am quiet, almost overwhelmed by the symbolism of flying a Spitfire from Biggin Hill over the green and pleasant land that Wellum, O'Neil and Bader et al fought over. I find it emotional and strangely tiring. Four combat sorties a day seems incomprehensible. We owe "The Few" so much.

Soon Biggin Hill is in sight and we need to do some manoeuvring to create air space and line us up for a landing. Don explains that the wind is coming across the field as we land so he will expertly land on the wheel nearest the wind first and then the second.

I would not have known had he not said as his flying was stunningly smooth.

We taxi, stop, get undone and shake hands. A few photos later and I am alone in the lounge, watching "my Spitfire" getting packed away for the night. I am exhilarated, moved, quiet, exhausted with adrenaline and pinching myself…. I have flown a Spitfire.

Thank you to Peter, Paul, James, the chap who made me tea and of course my pilot Don. I shall never forget today. Thank you for your polite, kind, professional organisation.

First Spitfire flight complete. *(Image: Greg Davis)*

Flight No.2: NH341

(18 September 2017)

I received an invite from *Aero Legends* to see NH341's new camera system in action. It would have been rude not to go and look!

"We wondered if you'd like to go up with Flight Lieutenant Antony *'Parky'* Parkinson in NH341 so that he can demonstrate NH341 and her camera system?" When you get a phone call like that then your heart rate increases, and you get a bit excited. Obviously, the answer was "Yes please!".

The plan was that I would do a short flight with *Parky* and we would find some photogenic scenery to demonstrate NH341's £40,000 camera system. This is not the normal GoPro set up but a fully integrated system, with twin video recorders to reduce the chance of a video not recording. It has a forward facing "gun cam", a tail mounted external camera along with a passenger facing camera.

I arrived late in the afternoon at Headcorn to fly at the end of the day. NH341 was sat ticking on the grass after her day's exertions. *Parky* gleefully welcomed me! Gulp - I am actually going to fly with a BBMF pilot in a Spitfire over Kent. I was both excited and nervous- after all I now knew what a Spitfire felt like to fly in. The first time, I was naively innocent but this time I knew what to expect!

I did my safety briefing and was reminded about things like how to bail out and use the parachute and then Ben showed me the camera system and how to use the gun cam by "firing" the gun button. Wayne then strapped me in and *Parky* did what he does on every flight; he talked me through all the checks that he does and then we taxied to the end of the runway. After a power test, *Parky* rolled NH341 forward and then that deafening roar started in front of us. The Merlin threw us down the runway, and in what seemed like only a few feet, we were airborne.

I was still nervous, but the feeling of flying into a beautiful evening in a Spitfire was once again breath-taking! Is it humanly possible to ever get bored of these sensations and emotions?

Under the clouds! *(Image: Greg Davis)*

Some aerobatics over Kent with "Parky" in NH341. *(Image: Greg Davis)*

Parky set off towards Leeds Castle, which we then swooped in and "attacked" with our camera. Then we flew under a storm cloud and chased along the edge of silvery wispy clouds. *Parky* had obviously forgotten about the "short" bit of our flight and on we went, watching the wind farm at Dymchurch, seeing the sun on the Channel. I knew what was coming next- *Parky* came over the intercom. "You need to do a bit of aero, let's do a Victory roll." Part of me wanted to fly on gently and the other part of me thought "I may never be in a Spitfire again." The second thought won. *Parky* accelerated in a long sweeping curve and then stuck the nose up about 40 degrees. Now travelling at about 240mph, we inverted and started to fall out of the roll. Blooming brilliant, blooming scary, but wonderful all the same!

It was time to head back to Headcorn. Once again adrenaline coursed through me making me almost lightheaded. *Parky* touched NH341 back on to the grass. I asked for a couple of minutes alone in order to catch my breath.

I have flown in my second Spitfire, with *Parky*, upside down at 240 miles an hour! Life will never be the same again!

Flight No.3: SM520

(28 November 2017)

It was the last day of the 2017 Spitfire season, a wonderful winter's day, bright sunshine but crisply cold. I slowed my car in order to go through the tunnel at the Goodwood circuit; I had arrived at the *Boultbee Flight Academy* for the next chapter of my Spitfire journey.

Matt Jones welcomed me into Boultbee's luxurious offices, and I was given a much-needed mug of boiling tea! He explained that after I had gone through full SSAC training I would be taken up in SM520 by Wing Commander Jim Schofield. Tim, one of the Boultbee team, took me into the training room and once again I completed my Spitfire flight training. Their videos were excellent, and despite this being my third flight I still picked up more useful information. Training completed; Tim took me to get kitted up. Boultbee pride themselves on their safety kit. They use full RAF-style helmets, life jackets and GPS transponders for each passenger. This is because the *Boultbee Flight Academy* often fly over water.

Tim introduced me to Wing Commander Jim Schofield. Jim has an amazing flying record which has included being a test pilot on the F-35 Lightning. Jim talked through what I wanted to achieve during my flight. During my first flight I had wanted to fly a Spitfire over my house, in my second flight I did some aerobatics. In this flight I wanted to do better at taking control. My first attempt at taking control resulted in me porpoising the Spitfire and that was not exactly comfortable. I resolved to do better this time!

We taxied to the end of the Goodwood runway and then, once again, that massive growling din that is being sat behind a Merlin at take-off. This time I was calmer than on my previous flights. I am getting used to this lark! We rose into a stunning winter sky and I had a huge Spitfire smile. Having levelled off, Jim offered me control of SM520. "I have control!" I shouted. This time I did a better job and for a few minutes I flew a Spitfire. I will just say that again, "For a few minutes I flew a Spitfire." What a ridiculous and amazing thing to say!

Jim took control and we flew along the coast, over Bognor Regis etc. Looking out over the Channel from my vantage point was very moving. Those young lads who had to fly out over the sea every day have my greatest respect.

Greg taking off from Goodwood in SM520. *(Image: Greg Davis)*

Soon Goodwood House came back into view and we made our curved approach; curved so that you can see where you are going over the Spitfire's long nose. Jim landed her on the bumpy grass strip, and we taxied back. I wound open my canopy a bit to let some air in. Can it be true? I have taken control of this amazing machine! I have completed three Spitfire flights even though I am not a pilot. I felt like pinching myself.

When I got to the locker room I felt strangely moved by the experience. A different and more reflective feeling than my previous flights. Matt brought me another mug of steaming tea. What an amazing day this has been, and one never to be forgotten.

Thanking Wing Commander Jim Schofield for an amazing flight. *(Image: Greg Davis)*

Flight No.4: PV202

(17 July 2018)

Spitfire Formations. As I walked towards the Aero Legends dispersal hut at Headcorn, two Spitfires were in the circuit coming into land. This was going to be a special day – a formation of Spitfires!

I reported to reception and signed in. There were eight Spitfire passengers which meant that there would be four formations of two Spitfires. I was booked in for 4 pm. I was delighted to discover that I was booked to fly in PV202 (or *'Charlie Alpha'* after the last two letters in her civil registration G-CCCA) with Ft. Lt. Charlie Brown. This would be my fourth flight in my fourth different Spitfire along with my fourth pilot!

We went into the training room to do our safety training (again!) and we sat around the Griffon engine table. It is very impressive and must weigh a ton. I was then introduced to Roy Slim who I would be flying in formation with. Roy was going to fly in NH341 with *Parky*. Roy and I were like excited kids as we waited for our turn to come around.

Before our flight Charlie Brown, *Parky*, Roy and I met up with a map to discuss our route and plan. We agreed that we would take off, formate on each other and then head towards Capel le Ferne in order to fly over the Battle of Britain Memorial together. We then planned to separate and do our own thing as Roy had a longer flight than me.

Once again, I was strapped into a Spitfire and we carried out pre-flight checks along with a power test before turning onto the runway. Every time that Merlin roars and you are flung off down the runway it takes you by surprise. Geoffrey Wellum used to talk about the Spitfire flying him in the early days and as she charges down the grass, eager to get into the sky, you kind of know what he meant!

Charlie look off to the west, however, we needed to head east and so he immediately did a 180-degree bank and we established level flight. Soon *Parky* and Roy caught us up and joined Charlie and I on the starboard side. I could not help but smile at the madness of the situation. Here was I, a non-pilot, bobbing along next to another Spitfire.

Taking off from Headcorn. *(Image: Roger Barrett)*

In formation and on the way to Capel le Ferne, Kent. *(Image: Greg Davis)*

Roy and I grinned and waved and even mouthed "Wow" etc to each other. Parky and Charlie manoeuvred *Charlie-Alpha* and *Elizabeth* around each other until we had each flown on the port and starboard sides and tail chased over the Kent countryside down to the coast. As we approached the Channel, we flew side by side in a banking turn over the Battle of Britain Memorial at Capel le Ferne. To fly in a formation of Spitfires over that memorial is possibly just about as good as it gets. Utterly stunning, beautiful, exciting, humbling, thrilling and unforgettable!

Parky and Roy carried on along the coast and Charlie and I headed for home. Once again, I became quiet in the back of a Spitfire. Flying back home at a couple of hundred miles an hour over Kent in the summertime is very moving. I mouth "Lest we forget" to the on-board camera, mainly to remind me of how I felt at this moment.

Capel to Headcorn is only eight minutes and soon Headcorn was in sight. We made the normal banked approached and touched down on the bumpy grass. Charlie wiped off our speed and we taxied back to the dispersal hut. I was exuberant, thrilled and grinning from ear to ear. Even if I never fly a Spitfire again, I will never forget the day I flew in this formation.

Flight No.5: MT818

(22 May 2019)

The phenomenal photoshoot! This is going to be a long one, so you will need to get yourself a coffee.

My phone rang on Tuesday evening and Peter Monk said, "We are doing something special tomorrow that you'll enjoy, can you get here?" Without even knowing what the "something special" was, I said yes! The next morning, I arrived at the *Biggin Hill Heritage Hangar* to find out what was going to happen. They were planning a complex photo-shoot that would require five pilots and four aircraft with the aim of capturing the three Spitfire Trainers! Then came the knockout question – which one would I like to fly in?!

I am sure I have had dreams where I was offered the choice of which Spitfire would I want to go up in but this time I was awake, and this was really happening! The choice was between MT818 – the only airworthy Spitfire Prototype in the world, MJ627 – a combat veteran (that I had already flown in), or MJ772 a D-Day veteran (in the 75th anniversary year). What a choice; what a decision to make!

Fortunately, I was going to have most of the day to decide as all the SSAC (customer) flights needed to happen before the photoshoot and, also, some of the pilots were still elsewhere in the country. Just then, ace aerial photographer, Richard Paver, arrived and over lunch explained that he hoped to do the photoshoot from an open door in the Airvan whilst wearing a harness that would attach him to the floor. Rather him than me! Hats off to Richard for his determination in order to get the perfect shot.

Several hours later, Richard Verrall called a planning meeting with all those who were involved. The Airvan was to be piloted by James Wood, accompanied by a second pilot Joe Hirst, who was to act as an additional lookout; a good idea in the circumstances.

- Spitfire 1 (MJ772), piloted by Don Signournay with Mark Britnell as passenger
- Spitfire 2 (MJ627), piloted by Dan Griffith with Richard Macintyre as passenger
- Spitfire 3 (MT818), piloted by Richard Verrall with yours truly as the passenger

The superb formation over Biggin Hill. *(Image: Richard Paver)*

Breaking left in MT818. *(Image: Richard Paver)*

The plan was that James would take the Airvan and Richard Paver (with harness!) up to the designated low population area. Don would then catch him up in MJ772 for a solo photo shoot. Phase two involved Dan joining the formation and Richard Paver would get MJ627 and MJ772 with their impressive invasion stripes. In phase three, Richard Verrall and I would join the formation to make up the three Spitfire Trainers in one formation photo. Finally, in phase four, each aircraft would break away from the formation one at a time.

Confession time: I am a bit of a nervous flyer and mention of the expression "break left" did nothing to calm my nerves. However, Richard Verrall, my pilot, has over 20,000 hours experience and has frequently flown royalty. So, if he says it will be OK, then it will be OK. We then proceeded to walk en masse to our waiting fleet of four aircraft.

The Airvan started up and departed, then Fred Mussard strapped me into my chosen Spitfire MT818. MJ772 then departed. MJ627 started and Richard fired up MT818. This was it – no turning back!

Everyone set off on their routes and MT818 taxied out on to the long empty expanse of the huge runway at Biggin Hill. The engine roared and that ridiculous shove in the back made me grin like a schoolboy! Within just a few hundred feet, we were airborne. After setting a course to vector in on our "target", three dots soon appeared, and we sneaked up behind them! We joined in on the extreme left and formed our row of three two-seat Spitfires. That is just a bonkers thing to say – we joined... a row of Spitfires!

James and Joe then led us through a choreographed series of turns. I have no idea how many times we turned and banked. On and on we went with Don, Dan and Richard fighting the natural bobbing of the air in order to hold our formation. We could see Richard Paver sitting in the open door of the Airvan, bright red harness in place. Using hand signals and radio commands, Spitfires 1, 2 and 3 were moved around with altitudes adjusted to meet the demands of the lens.

Eventually phase three's dizzy circus was complete and phase four began. The radio command was, "Spitfire No. 3, break left." A calm word from Richard Verrall and over we went, displaying our elliptical wings to the rest of the formation. Seconds later, MT818, Richard and I were on our way home. Biggin was soon in sight as we made the standard curved approach to the runway. So smooth was Richard's landing that I was unable to identify the moment that we went from aircraft to fast car. A sublime job. Canopy back, in order to get a breath of fresh exhaust fumes! After taxiing back, I unbuckled and thanked my superb pilot. A customary mug of steadying tea was required!

Blooming heck. Three of the most historic Spitfires have just flown circles all over North Kent – and I was in one of them! Exhausted as I was, sleep came slowly at night and was interrupted by the memorable sight in my mind of three swirling Spitfires.

To Peter Monk, who owns and maintains this mini air force, a sincere thank you. To everyone who helped in any way with an amazing day, thank you also. Thank you to all five pilots for their consummate skill and, especially, to Richard Verrall for helping this passenger through one of the best days ever!

The *Spitfire smile! (Image: Greg Davis)*

APPENDICES

This section of the book brings together a varied selection of information related to the two-seat Spitfire Trainer. It is provided here to add to the overall story of this previously sparsely documented variant.

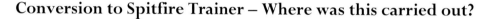

Conversion to Spitfire Trainer – Where was this carried out?

The question of where the conversion of Spitfires to Trainer status was carried out is not as easy to answer as you might think.

The formal conversions to two-seat configuration were carried out by the Supermarine division of Vickers-Armstrongs Ltd. between the years of 1946 and 1951. This was at a time when the whole UK aeronautical industry was dramatically winding down after World War II.

It has not been possible to determine precisely where the Spitfires were converted. The conversions were very much a 'cut and shut' affair requiring hands-on engineering in three small batches over several years, meaning they did not warrant a full production line.

A former Vickers employee of the time, Norman Parker, confirmed that MT818/G-AIDN (the prototype Spitfire Trainer), was converted in the experimental hangar at Hursley Park, near Winchester. It should be noted that Hursley Park was Vickers-Armstrongs Ltd.'s headquarters and not an airfield location. This conversion work would require a substantial assembly jig and fixture, securely bolted to the floor, not something easily moved. The final assembly and test flights for MT818 were conducted at High Post Airfield.

There is evidence from the South Marston dispatch book that the Spitfire Trainers destined for the Indian Air Force were shipped by road to Eastleigh Airfield for conversion. But were they converted at Eastleigh or were the fuselages shipped to Hursley Park to go into the fuselage jig? There is a good engineering case for them to be adjacent to the technical information and engineering staff for conversion in the Hursley Park experimental workshop hangar. It is confirmed that the three Dutch Spitfire Trainer conversions were dispatched to the Netherlands from Eastleigh Aerodrome, but some of the Irish Air Corps purchase documentation relates to Hursley Park.

Therefore, it may be speculated that both locations were involved, with the fuselage conversions being carried out at Hursley Park before dispatch to Eastleigh Aerodrome for final assembly and testing prior to delivery.

The experimental hangar at Vickers-Armstrongs headquarters, Hursley Park. Note camouflage pattern applied to exterior of building, to break up the outline from above, and the security fencing with guard posted outside. *(Image: Peter Arnold collection)*

The experimental workshop hangar at Vickers headquarters, Hursley Park. With no airfield facility, when necessary airframes were transported by road to various locations for final assembly and flight testing. *(Image: Peter Arnold collection)*

Vickers-Armstrongs Ltd Sales Brochure – Spitfire Trainer Conversions

Re-produced here in its entirety, the following pages show the brochure from Vickers-Armstrongs Ltd. created to support their efforts marketing and selling the Spitfire Trainer aircraft to Air Arms across the world.

Points to note when reading the document:

- Specification type numbers shown in this document, i.e. 499 & 502, were later changed to Type 502 and 509 for Mk.VIII and Mk.IX respectively.
- The fuel capacity of the production aircraft differs from this sales brochure.
  - Mk.VIII fuel tank capacity is 93 gallons, not 93½ as stated in this brochure. This consists of, Main tank: 39 gallons, Each wing: 1 off 14¼ gallon & 1 off 12¾ gallon.
  - Mk.IX fuel tank capacity is 90 gallons, not 94 as stated in this brochure. This consists of, Main tank: 38 gallons, Each wing: 1 off 13½ gallon & 1 off 12½ gallon.
  - To ensure accuracy, these figures have been confirmed against surviving aircraft.

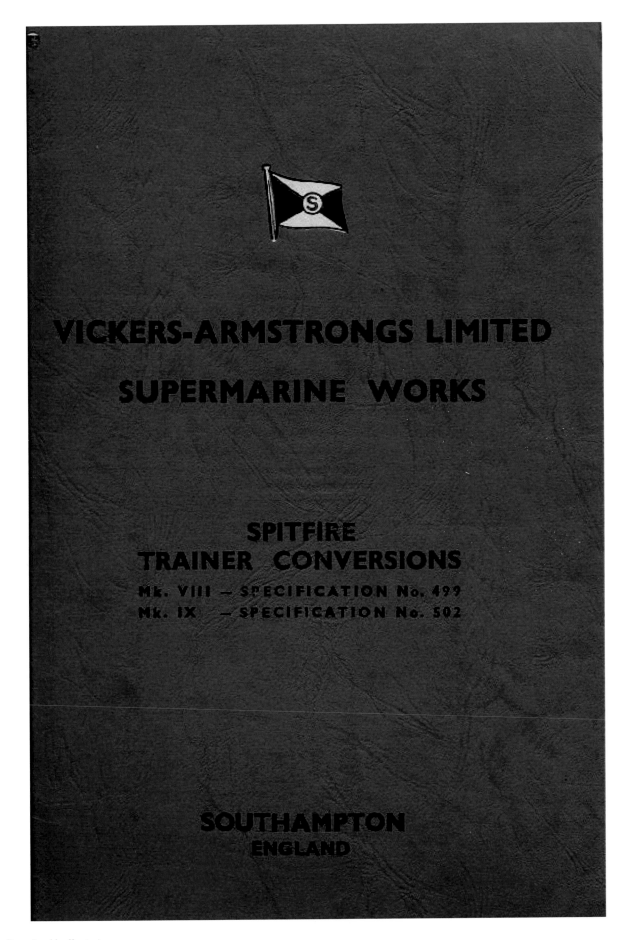

VICKERS-ARMSTRONGS LIMITED

SUPERMARINE WORKS

SPITFIRE
TRAINER CONVERSIONS
Mk. VIII — SPECIFICATION No. 499
Mk. IX — SPECIFICATION No. 502

SOUTHAMPTON
ENGLAND

(Peter Arnold collection)

SPITFIRE TRAINERS

(MK VIII & MK IX CONVERSIONS)

SPECIFICATION No. 499/502

VICKERS-ARMSTRONGS LIMITED

(Aircraft Section)

SUPERMARINE WORKS, SOUTHAMPTON

SPECIFICATION

No. 499/502 Issue 2

SPITFIRE HIGH PERFORMANCE TWO-SEAT TRAINERS

The Supermarine two-seat Trainers have been developed to fill a long-standing demand for a high speed single engine fighter trainer. The prototype aircraft is essentially a conversion from the famous Spitfire Mk. VIII, and faithfully retains the excellent handling characteristics of that aircraft. More-over, the considerable experience gained under wartime operational conditions enables all the best and proved features of the Spitfire to be blended into the outstanding trainer.

The COCKPITS are of conventional lay-out and the front cockpit, fully representative of an equivalent operational aircraft, is normally occupied by the pupil and is placed somewhat further forward (13½ ins.), than on the Spitfire.

The forward view from both cockpits is very good, and is obtained, in the case of the rear cockpit, by the instructor's seat position being raised above that of the front. Both cockpits have sliding and jettisonable hoods, the rear hood being of more bulbous shape to allow a forward view along the side of the front cockpit. All essential instruments and controls are faithfully duplicated.

FUEL is carried in the fuselage forward of the front cockpit, and tanks are also provided in each wing. For details of actual fuel tankage on the Mark VIII and Mark IX aircraft, reference should be made to the relevant general arrangement diagrams in this Specification.

For GUNNERY training four ·303 in. machine guns are provided, as well as a camera gun in the wing fillet.

BOMBING instruction is well catered for in these training aircraft with varying weight combinations. This aircraft is also approved for the carrying of Rocket Projectiles.

The ELECTRICAL SYSTEM derives its power from an engine driven generator charging a standard accumulator. A radio transmitter and inter-communication system, navigational and downward recognition lights are also fitted.

A complete OXYGEN SYSTEM is fitted as standard equipment.

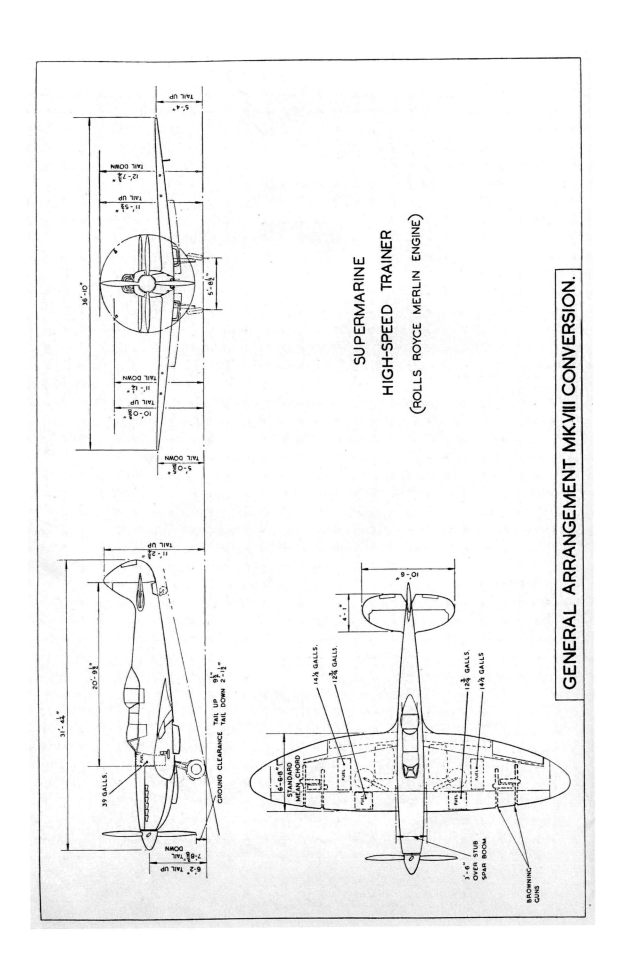

SUPERMARINE
HIGH-SPEED TRAINER
(ROLLS ROYCE MERLIN ENGINE)

GENERAL ARRANGEMENT MKVIII CONVERSION.

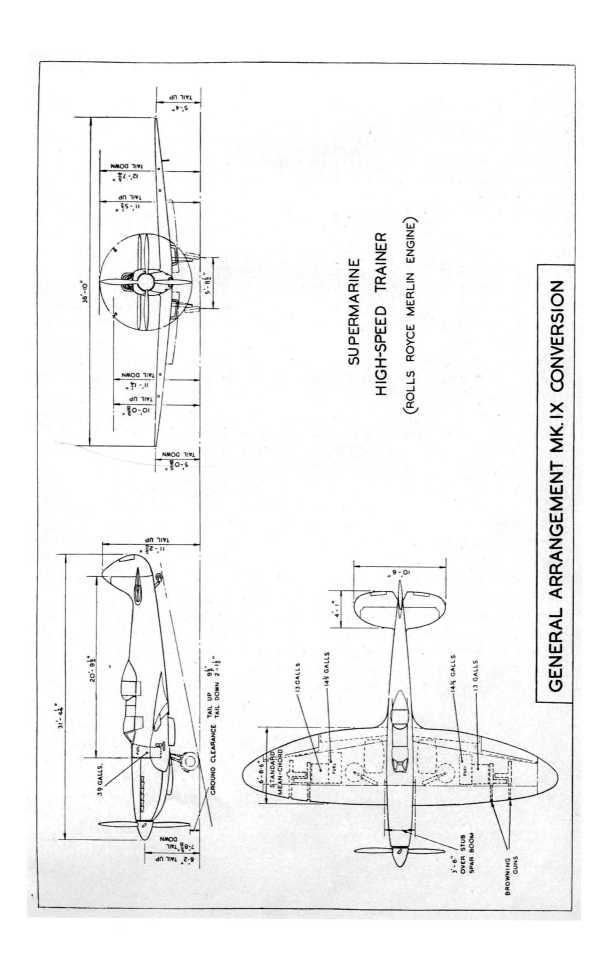

SUPERMARINE

HIGH-SPEED TRAINER

(ROLLS ROYCE MERLIN ENGINE)

GENERAL ARRANGEMENT MK.IX CONVERSION

152

SPITFIRE MK VIII TRAINER CONVERSION

LEADING PARTICULARS

DIMENSIONS
Span	36 ft. 10 in.	11·23 m.
Length	31 ft. 4¼ in.	9·56 m.
Maximum height. Tail down ..	12 ft. 7¾ in.	3·86 m.
Wing area	242 sq. ft.	22·48 sq. m.

WEIGHT AND LOADINGS
All-up weight. Normal ..	7,400 lb.	3,359·6 Kg.
Wing loading. Normal ..	30·6 lb./sq. ft.	1·495 Kg./sq. m.
Power loading	4·23 lb./b.h.p.	1·894 Kg./c.v.

ENGINE INSTALLATION
One Merlin 61, 63, 66, or 70 engine
One Rotol 10 ft. 9 in. dia. 4-blade constant speed propeller.

CAPACITIES
Fuel Tanks		Gallons	Litres
Total internal capacity		93½	425
Auxiliary jettisonable tank		30	136

PERFORMANCE DATA (MERLIN 66 ONLY)

(At Combat Power Rating)

Boost Pressure	67 in. Hg.	1,702 mm. Hg.

MAXIMUM SPEED
Fully supercharged at full throttle	393 m.p.h.	632 k.p.h.
height	20,000 ft.	6,100 m.
Moderately supercharged at full	362 m.p.h.	582 k.p.h.
throttle height..	9,000 ft.	2,745 m.
Moderately supercharged at sea level	326 m.p.h.	525 k.p.h.

RATE OF CLIMB
Fully supercharged at full throttle	3,890 ft./min.	1,186 m./min.
height	18,000 ft.	5,490 m.
Moderately supercharged at full	4,570 ft./min.	1,394 m./min.
throttle height..	7,000 ft.	2,135 m.
Moderately supercharged at sea level	4,540 ft./min.	1,385 m./min.

SERVICE CEILING 40,600 ft. .. .. 12,383 m.
i.e. height at which rate of climb is 100 ft./min.
(30·5 m./min.)

RANGE AND DURATION	Normal	With 30 Gall. Drop Tank	Normal	With 136 Litre Drop Tank
Average cruising speed..	232 m.p.h.	223 m.p.h.	373 k.p.h.	359 k.p.h.
Miles per gallon.. ..	6·51	6·25	—	—
Km. per litre	—	—	2·30	2·21
Duration of cruise (at 20,000 ft.) ..	1·03 hr.	1·87 hr.	1·03 hr.	1·87 hr.
Total distance (at 20,000 ft.)	240 miles.	418 miles.	386 Km.	673 Km.

The ranges quoted above include an allowance for take-off, climb to 20,000 ft. and fifteen minutes combat.

TAKE-OFF DISTANCE (At Normal All-up Weight)
Take-off distance to clear a 50 ft. (15·25 m.) obstacle in still air..	435 yds.	398 m.

7

SPITFIRE MK IX TRAINER CONVERSION
LEADING PARTICULARS

DIMENSIONS

Span..	36 ft. 10 in.	11·23 m.
Length	31 ft. 4¼ in.	9·56 m.
Maximum height. Tail down	12 ft. 7¾ in.	3·86 m.
Wing area ..	242 sq. ft.	22·48 sq. m.

WEIGHT AND LOADINGS

All-up weight. Normal ..	7,300 lb.	3,314 Kg.
Wing loading. Normal ..	30·17 lb./sq. ft.	147·44 Kg./sq. m.
Power loading ..	4·17 lb./b.h.p.	1·87 Kg./c.v.

ENGINE INSTALLATION

One Merlin 61, 63, 66, or 70 engine
One Rotol 10 ft. 9 in. dia. 4-blade constant speed propeller.

CAPACITIES

Fuel Tanks	Gallons	Litres
Total internal capacity ..	94	427
Auxiliary jettisonable tank	30	136

PERFORMANCE DATA (MERLIN 66 ONLY)

(At Combat Power Rating)

Boost Pressure ..	67 in. Hg.	1,702 mm. Hg.

MAXIMUM SPEED

Fully supercharged at full throttle height ..	386 m.p.h. 20,000 ft.	621 k.p.h. 6,100 m.
Moderately supercharged at full throttle height..	360 m.p.h. 9,000 ft.	579 k.p.h. 2,745 m.
Moderately supercharged at sea level ..	322 m.p.h.	518 k.p.h.

RATE OF CLIMB

Fully supercharged at full throttle height ..	3,970 ft./min. 18,000 ft.	1,211 m./min. 5,490 m.
Moderately supercharged at full throttle height..	4,650 ft./min. 7,000 ft.	1,418 m./min. 2,135 m.
Moderately supercharged at sea level ..	4,640 ft./min.	1,415 m./min.

SERVICE CEILING

41,500 ft.   12,658 m.
i.e. height at which rate of climb is 100 ft./min.
(30·5 m./min.)

RANGE AND DURATION

	Normal	With 30 Gall. Drop Tank	Normal	With 136 Litre Drop Tank
Average cruising speed..	228 m.p.h.	222 m.p.h.	367 k.p.h.	357 k.p.h.
Miles per gallon.. ..	6·40	6·23	—	—
Km. per litre	—	—	2·27	2·21
Duration of cruise (at 20,000 ft.)	1·03 hr.	1·86 hr.	1·03 hr.	1·86 hr.
Total distance (at 20,000 ft.)	234 miles	413 miles	377 Km.	665 Km.

The ranges quoted above include an allowance for take-off climb to 20,000 ft. and fifteen minutes combat.

TAKE-OFF DISTANCE (At Normal All-up Weight)

Take-off distance to clear a 50 ft.
(15·25 m.) obstacle in still air   430 yds.   393 m.

8

ENGINE PERFORMANCE DATA

ROLLS ROYCE MERLIN 66 (R.M. 10 S.M. RATING)   PROPELLER REDUCTION GEAR RATIO 0·477:1

	Boost lb./sq. in.	Boost in. Hg.	Boost mm. Hg.	R.P.M.	M.S. Gear Ht. in ft. B.H.P.	M.S. Gear Ht. in metres C.V.	F.S. Gear Ht. in ft. B.H.P.	F.S. Gear Ht. in metres C.V.
Take-off	+12	54	1,372	3,000	1,325	1,344	—	—
Combat Rating (for periods up to 5 minutes)	+18	67	1,702	3,000	5,500 ft. 1,750	1,678 m. 1,775	16,250 ft. 1,630	4,956 m. 1,653
International Rating (for periods up to 60 minutes)	+12	54	1,372	2,850	9,000 ft. 1,410	2,745 m. 1,430	19,000 ft. 1,315	5,795 m. 1,333

100/130 Grade (100 Octane) fuel must be used.

The figures quoted above relate to static conditions.

9

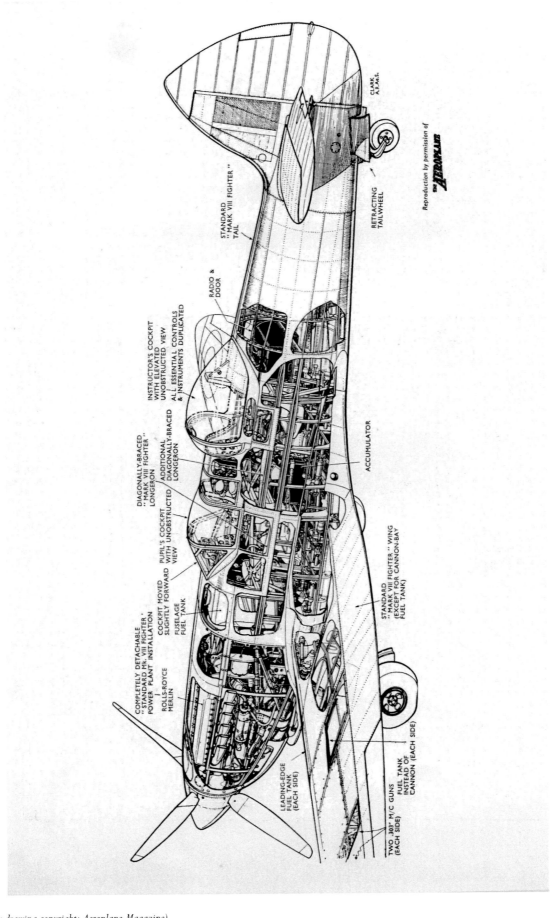

COMPLETELY DETACHABLE
"STANDARD MK. VIII FIGHTER"
POWER PLANT INSTALLATION

ROLLS-ROYCE
MERLIN

DIAGONALLY-BRACED
"MARK VIII FIGHTER"
LONGERON

COCKPIT MOVED
SLIGHTLY FORWARD

PUPIL'S COCKPIT
WITH UNOBSTRUCTED
VIEW

FUSELAGE
FUEL TANK

ADDITIONAL
DIAGONALLY-BRACED
LONGERON

INSTRUCTOR'S COCKPIT
WITH ELEVATED
UNOBSTRUCTED VIEW

ALL ESSENTIAL CONTROLS
& INSTRUMENTS DUPLICATED

RADIO &
DOOR

STANDARD
"MARK VIII FIGHTER"
TAIL

CLARK,
A.R.Ae.S.

RETRACTING
TAILWHEEL

ACCUMULATOR

STANDARD
"MARK VIII FIGHTER" WING
(EXCEPT FOR CANNON-BAY
FUEL TANK)

LEADING-EDGE
FUEL TANK
(EACH SIDE)

TWO .303" M/C GUNS
(EACH SIDE)

FUEL TANK
INSTEAD OF
CANNON (EACH SIDE)

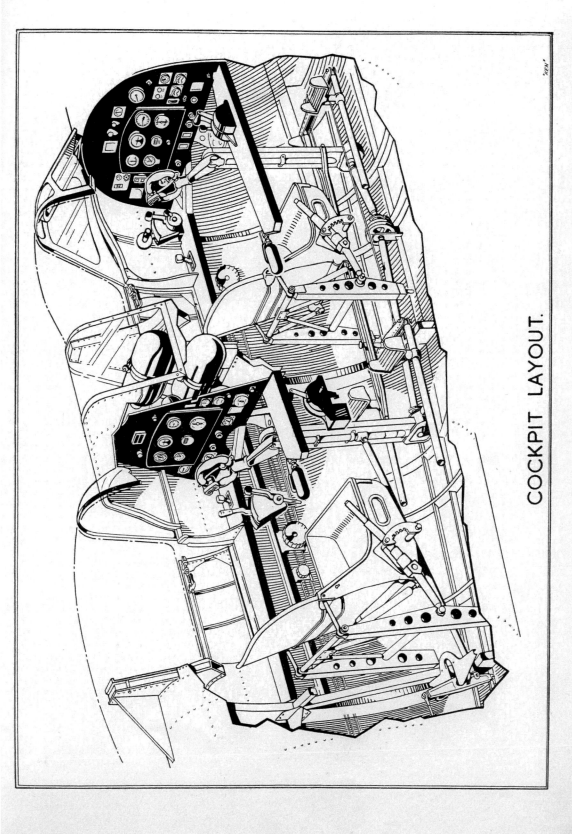

COCKPIT LAYOUT.

11

Printed in England by Sir Joseph Causton & Sons, Ltd., London and Eastleigh.

Prototype MT818 – A&AEE Handling Trials Report

As outlined earlier in the book, the prototype Spitfire Trainer (Mk.VIII MT818) was dispatched to the Aeroplane and Armament Experimental Establishment (A&AEE) at RAF Boscombe Down for handling trials in February 1947.

The full report from those handling trails is reproduced here. Positive points of note are the comparable performance of the Spitfire Trainer to the single-seat Spitfire Mk.VIII equivalent, and the improved visibility for take-off and landing from the front cockpit.

However, visibility from the rear cockpit for the instructor was noted as poor, and the aircraft was deemed as not suitable for gunnery training due to a lack of forward view from the rear cockpit.

The RAF did not place any orders for the Spitfire Trainer.

1ST PART/A.AE.E/692,Y.

W 043603

18 DEC 1947

MINISTRY OF SUPPLY

AIRCRAFT AND ARMAMENT

EXPERIMENTAL ESTABLISHMENT

BOSCOMBE DOWN

SPITFIRE TRAINER G-AIDN

(MERLIN 66)

BRIEF HANDLING TRIALS.

(Peter Arnold collection)

Unclassified.　　　　　　　　　　　1st. Part of Report No. A.&.E.E./692,y.

1 2 DEC 1947

AIRCRAFT AND ARMAMENT EXPERIMENTAL ESTABLISHMENT
BOSCOMBE DOWN.

Spitfire Trainer G-AIDN.
(Merlin 66)

Brief Handling Trials.

A.&.A.E.E. ref:- AAEE/5717,a/114/LRJ.
M.O.S.　　ref:- 7.Aircraft.1814.
Period of Tests:- Feb. - April,1947.

Summary.

The flying characteristics of the aircraft were found to be satisfactory
and similar to those of the basic Spitfire design from which it was converted.
The aircraft was considered a useful advanced flying trainer though the rear
cockpit was cramped and minor additional fitments were required.　It was also
found that the view from the rear cockpit, though restricted, was adequate for
giving flying instruction, but inadequate for air to ground gunnery instruction.

1.　Introduction.

Spitfire Trainer G-AIDN was sent to this Establishment for brief handling
trials and assessment as an advanced trainer.

The aircraft was a Spitfire Mk.VIII modified by the addition of a second
cockpit with dual control and the moving forward of the front cockpit by $13\frac{1}{2}$".

The results of the tests were sent by advance letter Ref: AAEE/5717,a/114/
LRJ dated 30th April,1947 to RDL1(a).

2.　Description of Aircraft.

2.1　General.

The aircraft was basically a Spitfire Mk.VIII modified by the fitting of
a second cockpit, dual control and the moving forward by $13\frac{1}{2}$" of the front
cockpit.　The rear cockpit was fitted with a sliding "bubble" canopy.

The forward movement of the front cockpit decreased the capacity of the
main fuselage fuel tanks but additional fuel tanks were fitted in the wings at
approximately the position normally occupied by the 20 m.m. guns on the Mk.VIII
as well as in the leading edges.

Four view photographs of the aircraft are attached.

The following were the main external features:-

Merlin 66 No. 179907/A479791

Rotal 4 bladed propeller.　Type R. 124F5/4 No. YA.7224.

Whip aerial behind rear cockpit.

2 x .303" guns in each wing.

Gun muzzles sealed, ammunition chutes open.

Mk.VIII pitot-static head under port wing.

2.2　Controls.

The tailplane and elevator were of the usual Mk.VIII plan form but the
elevator was metal-covered.　As a result of preliminary handling tests made
by the firm, $7\frac{3}{4}$" of angle metal were fitted above and below the trailing edge
on each side of the elevator adjacent to the central cut away.　The total

/thickness....

161

thickness across these angle strips when in position was ¾ ins.

In addition a 9½ lb. (88 lb.in.) inertia weight was fitted on the elevator control cross shaft behind the rear seat.

■ Elevator balance +80 lb.ins. } about elevator hinge.
   Inertia weight +88 lbins. }

Note x The out of balance moment of the elevator circuit, exclusive of the elevator itself and the inertia weight, was probably different to that of a standard Mk.VIII due to the additional control column. The moment has not been measured but the change was probably in the elevator up (-) direction, i.e. destabilizing.

The rudder was fabric-covered and was fitted with a trim tab, while the ailerons were metal-covered. Both controls were as for a standard Spitfire Mk.VIII.

2.3 Friction in Control Circuits.

The friction in the control circuits was measured with the controls moving slowly through their travels.

Elevator 2 - 3 lbs. (4)

Ailerons 2½ lbs. (2)

Rudder 4 lbs. (6)

The figures in brackets are the limits laid down in AP.970 Chapter 207 for an aircraft of this weight.

2.4 Flying Limitations relevant at time of tests :-

Maximum permissible speed (Service: 403 knots A.S.I.
                    (Civil: 348 knots A.S.I.

2.5 Loading.

The aircraft was flown at a take-off weight of 7510 lb. with C.G. at 7.4" aft of datum (undercarriage down).

3. Scope of Tests.

3.1 Brief handling tests were made to assess the flying qualities.

3.2 An assessment was also made of the suitability of the aircraft as an advanced trainer for flying and gunnery instruction.

4. Handling and Flying Qualities.

The following results are based on the aircraft being flown from the front cockpit.

4.1 Ground Handling.

The taxying and general ground handling characteristics were satisfactory and the oil and coolant temperatures remained within the permissible limits after 15 minutes taxying.

The view was found to be slightly better than for a normal Spitfire owing to the fact that the front cockpit was 1½"forward of the normal position.

4.2 Take-off and Initial Climb.

Take-offs were made with +12 lb/sq.in. boost and 3,000 rpm with flaps up,

/and.....

and half division nose-up elevator trim. The tail came up easily and there was only a slight tendency to swing to the left which could be corrected with rudder. The aircraft left the ground at approximately 75 knots A.S.I. When airborne, the controls were light and effective and there was no tendency for any overbalance to occur.

4.3 Climb.

In a climb at 145 knots A.S.I. from 4,000 - 8,000 ft. at +8 lb/sq.in. boost and 2850 rpm, the aircraft could be flown for short periods stick free. Climbing at these conditions was comfortable and the characteristics satisfactory.

4.4 Level Flight.

4.4.1. Slow Cruise.

At 182 knots A.S.I. at 5,000 ft. using zero boost and 2,000 rpm with rudder held fixed, after depressing the port wing approximately 15° and then releasing the stick the aircraft returned to normal in 6 - 5 secs; after similarly depressing the starboard wing and then releasing the stick the nose dropped and the aircraft entered a dive.

With wings held level, full rudder was applied in both directions and on releasing the rudder bar the aircraft returned to normal after 1 - 2 oscillations. In none of these tests was there any tendency for any control to overbalance.

4.4.2. Fast Cruise.

At 245 knots A.S.I. at 6,000 feet using +7 lb/sq.in. boost and 2650 rpm, the aircraft could be flown stick free in its trimmed state for long periods. With rudder held fixed and the port wing depressed 15°, the aircraft returned to normal in 7 - 3 seconds after release of the stick. When the starboard wing was depressed 15° and the stick released, the nose dropped and the speed increased to 260 knots A.S.I. before the aircraft returned to its trimmed speed a few seconds later.

With the wings held level, as much rudder as possible was applied in either direction and on release of the rudder bar the aircraft returned to normal in 3 - 4 oscillations.

4.5. Dives.

The following table gives the results of out-of-trim dives:-

Trimmed Speed.	Boost (lb/sq.in). R.P.M	Speed in Dive.	Push Force to Maintain dive.	'g' on release of stick Accelerometer reading.
A. 148 knots A.S.I.	+9 2850	295 knots A.S.I.	18 lb.	3.1 'g'
B. 278 knots A.S.I. Level.	+9 2850	368 knots A.S.I.	14 lb.	3.1 'g'
C. 193 knots A.S.I. Level.	0 2000	330 knots A.S.I.	20 lb.	3.4 'g'

The foot force in dive A was excessively high at 295 knots A.S.I. and had to be trimmed out, but was light in dive B.

4.6. Stalls.

Stalling speeds were:-

With both hoods closed   Flaps and undercarriage up   74 knots A.S.I.
                         Flaps and undercarriage down   65 knots A.S.I.

/With.....

With rear hood open   Flaps and undercarriage up   72 knots ASI.
                      Flaps and undercarriage down   65 knots ASI.

Warning of the stalls was given 2 - 3 knots before the stall by slight fore and aft oscillation of the stick.   The stall was accompanied by a straight nose drop. Recovery was readily effected when the stick was pushed forward.

4.7.   Aerobatics.

Aerobatics, including loops, rolls, upward rolls and half rolls off the top of loops, were carried out, there being sufficient power to execute all normal aerobatic manoeuvres at climbing power.

The aerobatic behaviour of the aircraft, when piloted from either cockpit was considered similar to that of a standard Spitfire at comparable weight.

4.8.   Landing and Baulked Landing.

Approach and landing was considered easier than normal owing to the better visibility given by the more forward cockpit as compared with a standard Spitfire.

With the aircraft trimmed to glide at 96 - 100 knots ASI with undercarriage and flaps down, the engine could be opened up to full take-off power (+12 lb/sq.in. boost and 3,000 rpm) and could be climbed away with a moderate push force on the stick and a moderately heavy foot force on the rudder.   There was ample time for the pilot to retrim.

5.   Suitability as a Trainer.

5.1.   Instructor in Rear Cockpit.

The instructor's view from the rear cockpit was bad at take-off until the tail was raised, and also was bad in the final stages of landing.   It was considered an experienced pilot should have no difficulty in giving flying instructions from the rear cockpit, and there was sufficient view for him to "save" a bad landing providing the intercom was working. For gunnery instruction the aircraft was considered unsuitable for air to ground training owing to the difficulty of judging heights at low altitude whilst diving, and owing to the absence of gun sights it would be unsuitable for air to air training.

When the aircraft was flown from the rear cockpit there was a tendency for the tail to be raised too high at take-off and care had to be taken otherwise there was a danger of the propeller hitting the ground.

5.2.   Layout of Cockpits.

The following adverse criticisms were made in respect of the front and rear cockpits:

Both cockpits were cramped, particularly the rear cockpit, which was considered too narrow even for a pilot of average build.

In the front cockpit the undercarriage control lever was set too close to the fuselage and this made selection difficult with gloves on.

In the rear cockpit the undercarriage control lever, together with the trimmer wheel, was almost out of reach.   The compass was very difficult to see, and the engine revolution counter was half hidden and difficult to see.

Provision for opening the hoods was merely by handgrips and it was considered winding mechanisms for both hoods were desirable.   The rear windscreen gives a very distorted view and this was embarrassing when landing with the rear hood closed. The rear hood cannot be opened or kept open whilst the front hood is closed.

Difficulty was experienced in entering the rear cockpit and it was considered a step should be incorporated.

The following equipment, which was not provided, was considered desirable in the rear cockpit:-

/Elevator.....

Elevator trimmer indicator.

Petrol cocks.

Magneto switches.

Friction clamp for throttle and propeller controls.

6.   Conclusions.

The flying characteristics of the aircraft were satisfactory and similar to those of the basic Spitfire design from which it was converted.

The aircraft was considered to be a useful advanced flying trainer, though the lack of forward view from the rear cockpit seriously restricted its capabilities as a gunnery trainer, in particular for air to ground firing.

Circulation List.

C.S. (A)
P.D.T.D.
D.A.R.D.
D.O.R.
D.M.A.R.D.
D.D.M.A.R.D.
D.D.A.R.D. (Airworthiness)
D.D.R.D. (Performance)
A.C.A.S. (T.R.)
D.D.A.P.9.
D.R.A.E.   11 copies.
D.Arm.R.D. (Air)
R.D.T.3.
A.D.R.D.L.1.   2 copies 1 for action.
B.L.E.U.
A.F.E.E.
T.F.2.
C.I. Accidents
R.D.T. Accidents
D.P.A.
O.C. Handling Sqdn.
R.T.P. (TIB)   55 copies.
R.T.O. Vickers Armstrong.   2 copies.

An Egyptian Mystery – By Peter Arnold

By the start of the 1980s, the number and the identity of all the Vickers built Type 502 and Type 509 Spitfire Trainers were pretty much in place. The prototype, the sales to the Royal Netherlands Air Force, the Indian Air Force, the single example for the Egyptian Air Force and the Irish Air Corps were all documented in the book 'Supermarine Aircraft since 1914' (published by Putnam & Company, 1981).

This book was written by C.F. Andrews and E.B. Morgan, both of whom worked in the library department at Vickers. Although they acknowledged that compiling the Class B Registrations allotted to all Vickers aircraft including the Spitfire Trainers had been extremely difficult, their listing was comprehensive... but not complete. The listing terminated with an undated entry of G.15-253 for a Hovercraft. There was no record of a further five (5) Spitfire Mk XIXs supplied by Airwork General Trading for the Indian Air Force in February 1953 or indeed for G.15-256 a further Spitfire Mk.XIX noted in the logbook of Airwork test pilot Sqn. Ldr. Tyszko on 19 March 1954.

A Class B Registration is a means by which manufacturers can fly and test civil and foreign military aircraft without a full civil registration. Vickers were allotted G.15 numbers and it was noted that, in their listing, no entry could be found for G.15-74 or G.15-75. This gap followed on from a batch of twelve (12) Mk.XIX Spitfires destined for the Indian Air Force through to mid-1949. There was

a further gap in the listings, G.15-80 and G.15-81, that fell between batches of Sea Otters destined for the Netherlands Navy and 'Indo-China' in mid-1950.

It was therefore a surprise when in 2005, aviation historian and journalist Phil Jarrett produced a couple of quality images of a two-seat Spitfire in primer bearing the fuselage serial G.15-75. How could this be, they were all apparently previously accounted for.

A follow up discussion with David Nicolle, a specialist in Middle-East aviation history, elicited the fact that in his discussions and correspondence with Egyptian Spitfire pilots there was mention of more than one Spitfire Trainer and an Egyptian Force serial of '670' was proffered. The evidence was a little thin but with no other visible alternatives recording a further sale, the Egyptians were the logical recipients.

In 1973 when I was just starting to gather parts for my Seafire Mk.46 project LA564, I enquired at Vickers South Marston if they had any technical details on my Seafire. A former inspector nearing retirement, but who had worked at South Marston since WWII, invited me to the airfield to view the spot where my Seafire would have been anchored down for engine runs. He also told me that he had the original handwritten aircraft dispatch register for South Marston which mentioned flights of my Seafire. This was all in pre-photocopier days, but I was able to photograph the entire register, including the pages reproduced here.

G.15-70	Spitfire PR.XIX N/K	Indian AF	HS701	u/d	24.5.49
G.15-71	Spitfire PR.XIX N/K	Indian AF	HS702	d/d	1.6.49
G.15-72	Spitfire PR.XIX N/K	Indian AF	HS703	d/d	8.6.49
G.15-73	Spitfire PR.XIX PK330?	Indian AF	HS704	d/d	23.6.49
G.15-74					
G.15-75					
G.15-76	Sea Otter ASR.I JN107	R Netherlands Navy	18-4	d/d	18.11.49
G.15-77	Sea Otter ASR.I JN141	R Netherlands Navy	18-5		19.1.50
G.15-78	Sea Otter ASR.I JN142	R Netherlands Navy	18-6	d/d	12.5.50
G.15-79	Sea Otter ASR.I JN186	R Netherlands Navy	18-7		Unconfirmed
G.15-80	Not known				
G.15-81	Not known				
G.15-82	Sea Otter ASR.I JM797	Indo-China	N-82		25.4.50
G.15-83	Sea Otter ASR.I JM741	Indo-China	N-83		28.4.50
G.15-84	Sea Otter ASR.I JM953	Indo-China	N-84		26.5.50

Extract from book 'Supermarine Aircraft since 1914' showing the gaps in Class B registrations.

Type	Engine Type	Serial No	Signal Dates	Allotment	Date of Dispatch	Pilot	Remarks
SEAFIRE 47 VP 462.	G88	16828-591615	39/4/48	Rolls Royce Hucknall CSA/129/48	11/5/48	LT. ASTARTON	
SPITFIRE 9. ML 113				V.A. Eastleigh	7/5/48	By Road	For conversion to trainer
SPITFIRE 9. MK 176				V.A. Eastleigh	10/5/48	" "	" "
SPITFIRE 9 MK 177				V.A. Eastleigh	11/5/48	" "	" "
MJ 518				V.A. Eastleigh	11/5/48	" "	" "
SPITFIRE 9 MJ 276				V.A. Eastleigh	11/5/48	" "	" "
SPITFIRE 9 NH 424				V.A. Eastleigh	12/5/48	" "	" "
SPITFIRE 24 VN 479	G61	6536-485781	30/3/48	6MU. Brize Norton 416/5408	31/5/48	F/O HUNTER	Cryptech + batteries exchanged
SPITFIRE 9 MH 432				V.A. Eastleigh	13/5/48	By Road.	For conversion to trainer
SPITFIRE 9 ML 417				V.A. Eastleigh	25/5/48	" "	" "
SPITFIRE 9 MJ 451				V.A. Eastleigh	26/5/48	" "	" "
SPITFIRE 9 MK 172				V.A. Eastleigh	24/5/48	" "	" "
SPITFIRE 9 MK 298				V.A. Eastleigh	24/5/48	" "	" "
SEAFIRE 47 VP 463	G89	20056-486097	30/4/48	V.A. Chilbolton CSA-RARA/1058/48	3/6/48	F/L Colquhoun	
SEAFIRE 47 VP 464	G88	20053-486094	30/4/48	V.A. Chilbolton CSA-RARA/1058/48	3/6/48	S/L MORGAN	
SPITFIRE TRAINER G-15-2	M66	181239-480457		V.A. Eastleigh	3/6/48	M' HILLWOOD	Was sent here for storage, now returned to Eastleigh for extra mods.
SPITFIRE 22 PK 603	O61	16544-485685		39 MU. Colerne 416/8470	7/6/48	F/O HUNTER	
SPITFIRE 22 PK 502	C61	16740-486783		39 MU. Colerne 416/8470	7/6/48	F/O HUNTER	
SPITFIRE 22 PK 524	G61	3946-520489		39 MU. Colerne 416/8470	7/6/48	F/O HUNTER	

Images of the handwritten dispatch logs from South Marston, detailing the twelve Spitfire Mk.IX aircraft sent to Eastleigh by road for conversion to Trainer status. *(Images: Peter Arnold)*

Type	Engine Type	Serial No	Signal Dates	Allotment	Date of Dispatch	Pilot	Remarks
SPITFIRE 9 MJ 794				V.A. Eastleigh	8/6/48	BY ROAD	
SPITFIRE 22 PK 481	G61	3716-580471		39 MU. Colerne 416/8494	11/6/48	F/O HUNTER.	Batteries + cryptech received.
SEAFIRE 47 VP 431	G88	17206-599812	31/5/48	RNAS ANTHORN RARA/162/48	21/6/48	LT. WATERS	
SEAFIRE 47 VP 438	G88	17219-599815	31/5/48	RNAS ANTHORN RARA/171/48	21/6/48	LT. GREEN	
SEAFIRE 47 VP 465	G88	17162-599831	31/5/48	RNAS ANTHORN RARA/158/48	21/6/48	LT. SADBRIDGE	
SEAFIRE 47 VP 473	G88	17204-599811	31/5/48	RNAS ANTHORN RARA/172/48	22/6/48	LT. Astarton	
WELLINGTON X MERCURY NA 912			30/6/48	12 MU. Kirkbride	1/7/48		
SEAFIRE 47 VP 475	G88	17176-599797	30/6/48	RNAS ANTHORN RARA/186/48	2/7/48	LT. COWLING.	
SEAFIRE 47 VP 478	C88	20092-485133	30/6/48	RNAS ANTHORN RARA/186/48	2/7/48	LT. WILCOX	
SEAFIRE 47 VP 474	C88	17170-599794	30/6/48	CSA 00/45/48 RARA/106/48 V.A. Chilbolton	2/7/48	F/L COLQUHOUN	
SPITFIRE 22 PK 384	G61	16500-486663	29/6/48	39 MU. Colerne 416/8593	5/7/48	F/O HUNTER.	
SPITFIRE 22 PK 602	G61	5874-520453	30/6/48	39 MU. Colerne 416/8556	5/7/48	F/L CLYMO	
WELLINGTON X MERCURY NA 981			30/6/48	12 MU. Kirkbride	6/7/48	S/L KIRBY.	
SEAFIRE 47 VP 480	G88	17172-599795	30/6/48	RNAS ANTHORN RARA/196/48	8/7/48	LT. WILCOX	
SEAFIRE 47 VP 479	C88	17320-599869	30/6/48	RNAS ANTHORN RARA/196/48	8/7/48	LT. BRENNER.	
SEAFIRE 47 VP 477	G88	20073-486113	30/6/48	RNAS ANTHORN RARA/196/48	8/7/48	LT. COWLING.	

The log recorded, and I have highlighted, the dispatch of twelve (12) Mk IX Spitfires from Vickers South Marston to Vickers-Armstrongs at Eastleigh by road for the express purpose "for conversion to trainers".

Analysis of these twelve serials reveals that nine were latterly converted for the Indian Air Force, to be joined by MA848 already at Eastleigh, to complete the order of ten. Of the three other serials MJ794, ML113 and NH424, one (ML113) was ascribed by Andrews/Morgan as company demonstrator *G.15-92*, which went on to become G-ALJM and *684* of the Egyptian Air Force, being delivered 13 April 1950. It is noted that serial *684* sits squarely in the middle of the Mk.22 Spitfires sold to Egypt in 1950 in the range *681* to *689* and respectively *G.15-88* to *G.15-107*.

So, we have two Mk.IX Trainers, MJ794 & NH424 both assigned to trainer conversion by Vickers South Marston, we have one mystery two-seat Spitfire marked *G.15-75*, we have a missing slot in the Andrews/Morgan list for the adjacent *G.15-74* and *G.15-75* and we have the Nicolle research indicating that there was more than one Spitfire Trainer operated by the Egyptian Air Force. The delivery dates of the adjacent Class B registrations to this pair indicate that they, or it, would have been delivered some seven to eleven months before the arrival of the first Spitfire Mk.22 to Egypt, which is an appropriate time for a training programme.

Whilst this is not evidence beyond reasonable doubt, it is certainly a strong case for the Egyptians receiving not one but possibly three (3) Spitfire Trainers.

Spitfire Trainer *G.15-75* in the UK circa August 1949. *(Image: Phil Jarrett collection via Peter Arnold)*

Spitfire Trainer Order/Delivery Analysis

The table below shows all Vickers-Armstrongs Ltd converted Spitfire Trainer aircraft. It outlines the correlation between RAF serial number and Class B registration where confirmed, along with dates of purchase through to onward delivery.

Mark	RAF Serial	Class B Registration	Reg.	Sold to VA	Registered	First flight	Depart South Marston [1]	Despatch Book Remarks [2]	Delivery date	Air Force	Air Force Serial	Comments
VIII	MT818	N-32	G-AIDN	Feb-45	22-Aug-46	09-Sep-46						Prototype
VIII	unknown		G-AKBD		14-Jul-47							Withdrawn 31 May 1948
IX	MK715	N-41		02-Jan-47					23-Mar-48	Netherlands	H-97	
IX	BS274	N-42		11-Jan-47					23-Mar-48	Netherlands	H-98	
IX	BS147	G.15-1		02-Jan-47					23-Mar-48	Netherlands	H-99	
IX	MA848	G.15-2		22-Jan-47					03-Jun-48	Indian	HS534	
IX	MH432	G.15-3		17-Oct-46			13-May-48	For conversions to trainers	Sep-48	Indian	HS535	
IX	MJ177	G.15-4		16-Apr-47			11-May-48	For conversions to trainers	29-Sep-48	Indian	HS536	
IX	MJ276	G.15-5		16-Apr-47			11-May-48	For conversions to trainers	29-Sep-48	Indian	HS537	
IX	MJ451	G.15-6		30-Oct-46			26-May-48	For conversions to trainers	Sep-48	Indian	HS538	
IX	MJ518	G.15-7		30-Nov-46			11-May-48	For conversions to trainers	Nov-48	Indian	HS539	
IX	MK172	G.15-8		21-Oct-46			24-May-48	For conversions to trainers	15-Nov-48	Indian	HS540	
IX	MK176	G.15-9		24-Oct-46			10-May-48	For conversions to trainers	15-Nov-48	Indian	HS541	
IX	MK298	G.15-10		31-Oct-46			24-May-48	For conversions to trainers	15-Nov-48	Indian	HS542	
IX	ML417	G.15-11		31-Oct-46			25-May-48	For conversions to trainers	15-Nov-48	Indian	HS543	
XIX		*G.15-73*							*23-Jun-49*			*Shown to highlight delivery date timeline*
IX	MJ794	*unknown*		17-Oct-46			08-Jun-48	none				*For further information relating to these aircraft and the unattributed Class B Regs see investigative piece 'An Egyptian Mystery' elsewhere in this book*
IX	NH424	*unknown*		02-May-47			12-May-48	For conversions to trainers				
unknown	*unknown*	G.15-74										
IX	*unknown*	G.15-75										
Sea Otter		*G.15-76*							*18-Nov-49*			*Shown to highlight delivery date timeline*
IX	ML113	G.15-92	G-ALJM	16-Oct-47	14-Mar-49		07-May-48	For conversions to trainers	13-Apr-50	Egypt	684	
IX	MJ627	G.15-171		19-Jul-50					05-Jun-51	Irish	158	
IX	MJ772	G.15-172		19-Jul-50					05-Jun-51	Irish	159	
IX	MK721	G.15-173		19-Jul-50					29-Jun-51	Irish	160	
IX	PV202	G.15-174		19-Jul-50					29-Jun-51	Irish	161	
IX	ML407	G.15-175		19-Jul-50					30-Jul-51	Irish	162	
IX	TE308	G.15-176		19-Jul-50					30-Jul-51	Irish	163	

Notes:
1. Date of departure from Vickers-Armstrongs Ltd. South Marston via road bound for Eastleigh for conversion to trainer.
2. Annotation in South Marston Despatch Book ('Remarks' column). See An Egyptian Mystery on the preceding pages for further details.

Spitfire Trainers – RAF Squadron Service

Table below provides a summary view of RAF squadron service for all known Spitfire Trainer aircraft.

RAF Serial

Sqn	BS147	BS274	BS410	BS548	EN179	EN570	ES127	MA848	MH367	MH432	MJ177	MJ276	MJ451	MJ518	MJ627	MJ772	MK172	MK176	MK298	MK715	MK721	ML113	ML407	ML417	MT818	NH341	PT462	PV202	SM520	TE308
4								x																			x			
33																												x		
65									x																					
129								x																						
130										x																				
131								x																						
132																						x								
165								x																						
222										x																				
229									x																					
253																											x			
261								x																						
306				x																										
308																			x	x										
310	x							x																						
312									x																					
315			x	x																										
316				x																										
322	x	x																x	x											
329																		x												
332																						x								
340				x							x			x		x														
341				x								x				x							x							
345																							x							
349																							x							
401	x									x											x			x						
402				x																	x									
411																			x				x			x				
412																			x				x					x		
414														x																
417								x																						
421											x																			
441												x			x								x							
442										x													x							
443													x										x							
453								x			x																			
485																		x					x							
504								x																						
602												x																		
611				x																										
Post RAF service	Netherlands	Netherlands						India		India	India	India	India	India	Ireland	Ireland	India	India	India	Netherlands	Ireland	Egypt	Ireland	India			Italy, Israel	Ireland	South Africa	Ireland
Comments			Warbird-era rebuild	Warbird-era rebuild	Warbird-era rebuild	Warbird-era rebuild	Mk V field conversion		Warbird-era rebuild												No Sqn service				Prototype. No Sqn service	Warbird-era rebuild	Warbird-era rebuild		Warbird-era rebuild. No Sqn service	No Sqn service

Spitfire Construction Numbers – By Peter Arnold

Here are a few words about Spitfire construction numbers…they are complex.

The main data plate for a Spitfire fuselage is small, carries no RAF serial link and is rivetted to the fuselage just below the datum longeron on the right-hand side of the cockpit.

If the Spitfire was built by Supermarine the construction number is prefixed with a '6S'. If, however the airframe was built at Castle Bromwich it is prefixed with 'CBAF', South Marston 'SMAF', Westlands 'WASP', Cunliffe Owen 'CO' etc. A further plate is rivetted to the fuselage firewall (Frame 5) and is the major assembly number for the freestanding firewall, many of which were subcontracted out.

Conventionally the firewall/front bulkhead is where many other manufactures would affix the main data plate but not so on the Spitfire and Seafire. That would be too simple.

When it came to the Spitfire Trainer conversions and the moving of the cockpit structure forward, the aircraft within the initial Indian order, all Castle Bromwich (CBAF) built Mk.IXs, were considered as new build airframes and reissued with new Supermarine (6S) data plates in both the cockpit and on the firewall.

In the one case where an ex Indian Air Force two-seat Spitfire, HS543, was returned to the UK to be converted back to a single-seat aircraft, by Personal Plane Services at Booker, it can be noted in the image below that this plate was allocated to the aircraft when she was converted to Type 509 Trainer status due to the number *50927*

which refers to Type 509 and group 27 which denotes fuselage.

At this time in the 1980s, and despite a rigorous search to find the RAF serial of this trainer, no clues could be found of her previous identity. As a speculative measure I said to then owner Stephen Grey how about we drill the rivets on the firewall plate just in case there is anything written on the back…and sure enough there was, ML417, her RAF identity.

Following a later change in Vickers policy, the order for the Irish Air Corps quote the original build CBAF construction numbers in all of the delivery and release documentation for the individual Spitfires.

The construction numbers quoted in the Civil Aviation Authority (CAA) registration documentation for MT818/G-AIDN and G-AKBD, 6S/729058 & 6S/730847 respectively, are a long way out from the original build sequence if we use known Spitfire survivor MT719 (6S/442296) as a guide. This indicates that MT818/G-AIDN was renumbered as a new aircraft when she underwent conversion in August 1946.

Firewall plate from ML417 showing new '6S' conversion construction number. It was on the reverse of this plate that the original RAF serial was found. *(Image: Peter Arnold)*

Irish Air Corps – Delivery and Sales Information

As you will have read earlier in the book, the Irish Air Corps operated six (6) Spitfire Mk.IX Trainer aircraft. These aircraft were all converted from single-seat airframes by Vickers-Armstrongs Ltd., purchased by the IAC, and delivered to Baldonnel by the end of July 1951. The aircraft were used as advanced trainers, with one (MK721/IAC 160) being unfortunately written off in an accident, before being retired and going on to serve as instructional airframes.

Two (2) of the aircraft were put up for sale in 1963, with the final three (3) offered in 1968. The table below shows the delivery and sale for each of these aircraft.

Serial		Delivery date	Sale date	Comments
MJ627	(158)	5 June 1951	13 November 1963	Purchased by John Crewdson (Film Aviation Services Ltd.)
MJ772	(159)	5 June 1951	5 November 1963	Purchased by John Crewdson (Film Aviation Services Ltd.)
MK721	(160)	29 June 1951	n/a	Crashed 15 February 1957. Written off
PV202	(161)	29 June 1951	4 March 1968	Purchased by Anthony Samuelson (Samuelson's Film Services)
ML407	(162)	30 July 1951	4 March 1968	Purchased by Anthony Samuelson (Samuelson's Film Services)
TE308	(163)	30 July 1951	4 March 1968	Purchased by Anthony Samuelson (Samuelson's Film Services)

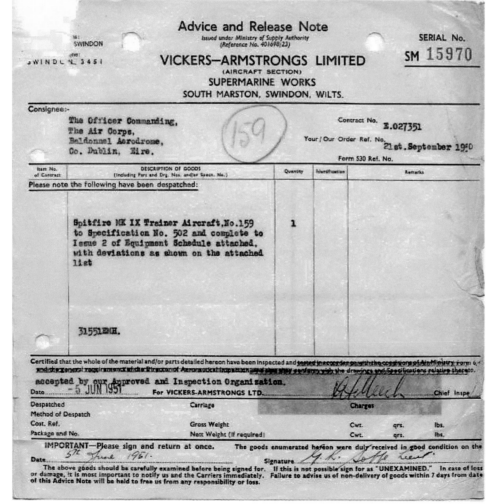

Delivery note for Spitfire Trainer MJ772 (IAC 159) to the Irish Air Corps at Baldonnel on 5 June 1951. *(Image: Tony Kearns via Peter Arnold collection)*

Above: Documentation inviting tenders for the sale of Spitfire Trainers 161, 162, & 163 (PV202, ML407, & TE308 respectively). *(Image: Tony Kearns via Peter Arnold collection)*

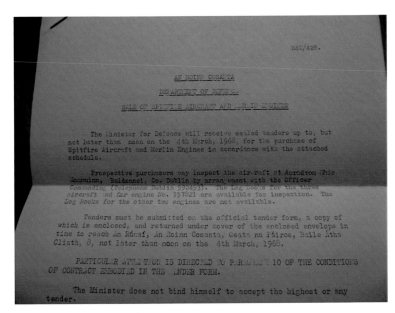

Left: Extract from above documentation, providing greater detail of the aircraft and engines on offer. Note, TE308 was sold as an airworthy aircraft, whilst both PV202 & ML407 were in a dismantled state. *(Image: Tony Kearns via Peter Arnold collection)*

When is a Spitfire Trainer, not a Spitfire Trainer?

During our research we have come across references erroneously declaring certain Spitfire aircraft as having undergone conversion to two-seat Trainer status. In addition, there are other Spitfire aircraft that were planned to be converted but were not.

In the interests of accuracy and completeness, we outline the aircraft here for the benefit of future researchers.

Spitfire Trainers that never were

The well-respected book 'Spitfire: The History' *(Published by Key Books, 2000)* by authors Eric Morgan and Edward Shacklady is a wealth of information regarding the Spitfire direct from the Vickers-Armstrongs Ltd. archives. However, during our research we uncovered mention of several aircraft that are purported to have undergone conversion to Spitfire Trainer configuration which did not.

The extract shown below, from page 377 of the book, offers a list of aircraft converted to two-seat Trainer configuration. Whilst the majority included in the list concur with our research, there are a few (outlined below in red), which were not converted and remained as single-seat aircraft.

On the following pages we provide information to debunk these erroneous entries in order that they do not perpetuate as fact by future researchers.

TA858, TE133, 303, 308 and 568.

Two-seat Trainers: BS147, MA848, MH415, 432, 434, MJ177, 276, 451, 518, 627, 772, MK172, 196, 298, 715, 721, ML113, 345, 407, 417, PV202 and TE308.

USAAF: EN180, 183-185, 201, 207, 302, 345, 453, 463

Extract from 'Spitfire : The History' showing the list of conversions to two-seat status, including the erroneous entries highlighted in red.

MH415

MH415 is a surviving Mk.IX aircraft, following post-war service with the Netherlands and Belgian Air Forces, went on to feature in the movie *The Battle of Britain*. Sold to Wilson *'Connie'* Edwards, MH415 was shipped to the USA and flew for a few years before being placed in storage at her owner's ranch in Texas.

Many years later, MH415 was shipped to Australia for rebuild, a job undertaken at Pay's Air Service, Scone NSW. MH415 was shipped to Sywell Aerodrome, UK where she arrived in early March 2020.

MH415 has a proven single-seat history, therefore her inclusion in this listing is an error.

Wilson *'Connie'* Edwards flying MH415 over Texas during 1973. When Kay Arnold asked if his ranch was down there somewhere, he replied simply "Yep, that's all my ranch…". *(Image: Wilson 'Connie' Edwards via Peter Arnold collection)*

MK196

The inclusion of MK196 in the list of aircraft converted to two-seat status is an error and appears to be a simple typographical error. Worthy of note, proven Spitfire Trainer MK176 (See Royal Indian Air Force, HS541) is not included within the list, therefore this appears to be a simple mix-up between a '7' and a '9', and the entry should read '*176*' instead.

To support this conclusion, Spitfire Mk.IX MK196 served with the Armée de L'Air (French Air Force) and unfortunately suffered a fatal mid-air collision with MK686 on 17 February 1948. Sadly, her pilot, Cne. Wicker was killed. MK196 was declared Cat.E (write-off) and struck off charge.

ML345

ML345 was not converted to Spitfire Trainer configuration, she was however sold back to Vickers-Armstrongs Ltd in April 1947, which may have led to this erroneous conclusion. She was in fact sold on to the Royal Danish Air Force as an instructional airframe, i.e. not airworthy, and given the identity FMSm2.

ML345 was allocated to the School of Technical Training (SoTT) at Værløse, Denmark where she was used to train ground crew. She was later struck off charge and subsequently scrapped.

MH434

MH434 is also a surviving Mk.IX aircraft, and probably one of the most well-known Spitfires. She has appeared in many movies, including *The Battle of Britain*, along with numerous television shows whilst being flown over the years by the iconic father and son partnership, Ray and Mark Hanna.

MH434 is based at Duxford Airfield in Cambridgeshire and operated by The Old Flying Machine Company. Another aircraft with a proven single-seat history, the inclusion of MH434 in this listing is an error.

MH434 on static display before the Battle of Britain Airshow at Duxford Airfield on 21 September 2019. *(Image: Peter Arnold)*

One of our aircraft is missing…

Worthy of note is the omission from the list of the third proven Royal Netherlands Air Force Spitfire Trainer aircraft, Mk.IX BS274/H-98. She is detailed earlier in this book *(see Royal Netherlands Air Force, BS274)*, and is a confirmed conversion to two-seat configuration.

However, whilst BS274 is mentioned within 'Spitfire: The History' in the Mk.IX chapter *(as 'BF274')* reflecting her career as a trials aircraft, she does not get an individual aircraft entry summarising her history.

Spitfire Trainers that were planned but never materialised

Spitfire Mk.IX MJ271, or *The Silver Spitfire* as she is better known, famously undertook an incredible trip to circumnavigate the globe during 2019.

Piloted by Matt Jones, Steve Brooks and former Battle of Britain Memorial Flight commanding officer Ian Smith,

MJ271 departed Goodwood Aerodrome on 5 August 2019. She flew approximately 27,000 miles over 22 countries, before her return to Goodwood on 5 December 2019. Simply an incredible achievement.

For more information visit www.silverspitfire.com

MJ271 (G-IRTY) after completion of rebuild at Duxford Airfield on 13 July 2019. *(Image: Peter Arnold)*

MJ271, '*The Silver Spitfire*', touches down at Goodwood Aerodrome on 5 December 2019 following her epic round the world adventure. *(Image: Roger Barrett)*

However, what is not so widely known is that she was very nearly converted to Spitfire Trainer status. Following acquisition by the *Boultbee Flight Academy* in August 2016, the original intention was for MJ271 to be rebuilt as a two-seat aircraft and join Boultbee's stablemate Spitfire Trainer Mk.IX SM520 at Goodwood Aerodrome. This initial intention was later withdrawn and MJ271 remained a single-seat aircraft. She was restored at Duxford by *Historic Flying Ltd* with a first post restoration flight on 27 June 2019. MJ271 was finished in a non-military scheme with highly polished skins wearing her civilian registration G-IRTY along her fuselage and was then prepared for her epic journey.

The images below are extracts from the contract placed by the *Boultbee Flight Academy* with *Historic Flying Ltd.* to convert MJ271 to two-seat Trainer configuration.

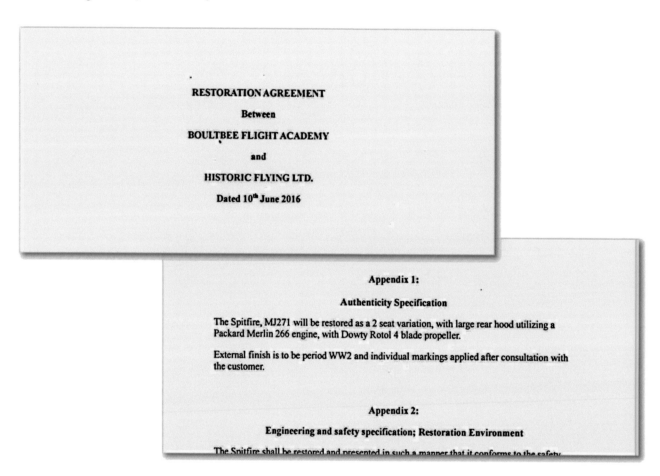

RESTORATION AGREEMENT

Between

BOULTBEE FLIGHT ACADEMY

and

HISTORIC FLYING LTD.

Dated 10th June 2016

Appendix 1:

Authenticity Specification

The Spitfire, MJ271 will be restored as a 2 seat variation, with large rear hood utilizing a Packard Merlin 266 engine, with Dowty Rotol 4 blade propeller.

External finish is to be period WW2 and individual markings applied after consultation with the customer.

Appendix 2:

Engineering and safety specification; Restoration Environment

The Spitfire shall be restored and presented in such a manner that it conforms to the safety

Above: Extracts from contract placed by *Boultbee Flight Academy* with *Historic Flying Ltd.* to rebuild MJ271 in Spitfire Trainer configuration. *(Extracts kindly provided by Matt Jones/Boultbee Flight Academy)*

MJ271 was displayed, albeit static only, at the Duxford Spitfire Airshow on 3 September 2006. Although she is an ex. Royal Netherlands Air Force machine, the markings MJ271 wears here are spurious. *(Image: John Sanderson)*

MJ271 in the jig at Historic Flying Ltd., Duxford Airfield, 11 March 2017. *(Image: Richard Paver)*

Logbook extracts from surviving Spitfire Trainers

In this chapter we present significant extracts from both pilot and aeroplane logbooks.

MT818

The first, 15-minute, flight of MT818 (G-AIDN) following her conversion to two-seat configuration on 9 September 1946 is recorded within her logbook and highlighted in the extract shown below. *(Logbook extract kindly provided by Richard Paver)*

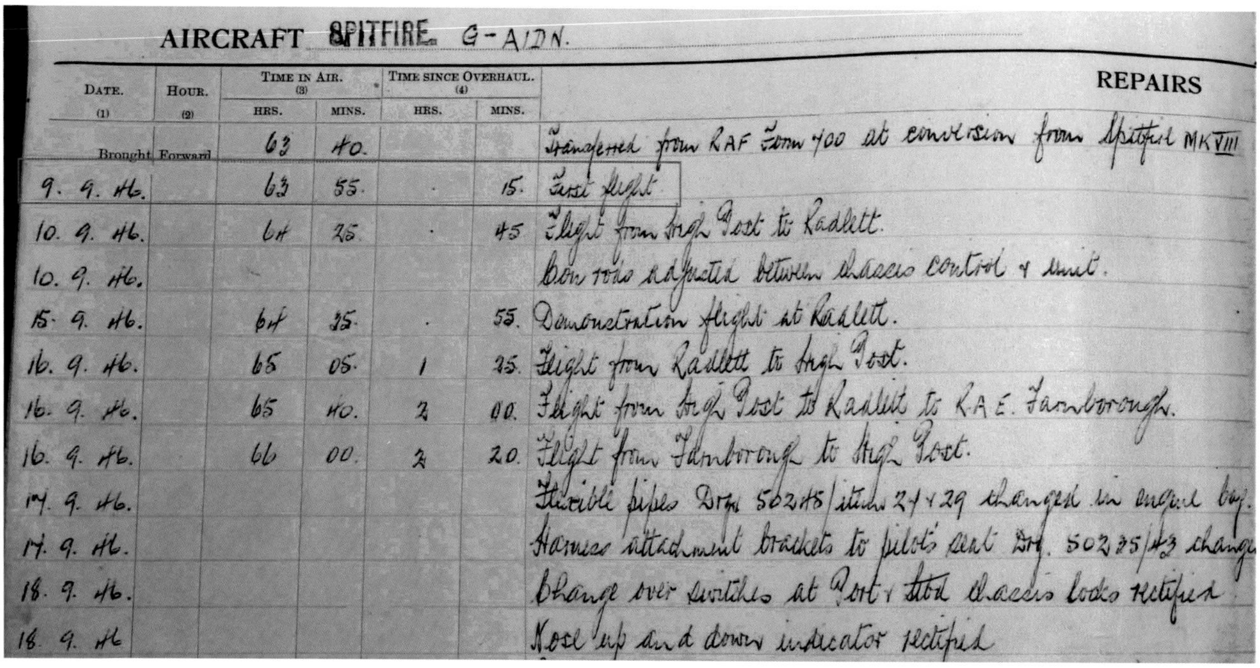

AIRCRAFT SPITFIRE G-AIDN.

DATE. (1)	HOUR. (2)	TIME IN AIR. (3) HRS.	MINS.	TIME SINCE OVERHAUL. (4) HRS.	MINS.	REPAIRS
Brought Forward		63	40.			Transferred from RAF Form 700 at conversion from Spitfire MK VIII
9. 9. 46.		63	55.	.	15.	First flight
10. 9. 46.		64	25.	.	45	Flight from High Post to Radlett.
10. 9. 46.						Bow rods adjusted between chassis control & unit.
15. 9. 46.		64	35.	.	55.	Demonstration flight at Radlett.
16. 9. 46.		65	05.	1	25.	Flight from Radlett to High Post.
16. 9. 46.		65	40.	2	00.	Flight from High Post to Radlett to R.A.E. Farnborough.
16. 9. 46.		66	00.	2	20.	Flight from Farnborough to High Post.
17. 9. 46.						Flexible pipes Drg 50248/items 27 & 29 changed in engine bay.
17. 9. 46.						Harness attachment brackets to pilot's seat Drg. 50235/43 changed
18. 9. 46.						Change over switches at Port & Std chassis locks rectified
18. 9. 46						Nose up and down indicator rectified

Wartime Polish fighter pilot, and later world-renowned test pilot, Janusz 'Zura' Żurakowski flew the prototype Spitfire Trainer MT818 on 4 March 1947 (a few short months after her first flight in September 1946) as highlighted in the extract below from his logbook. *(Logbook extract kindly provided by Wojtek Matusiak)*

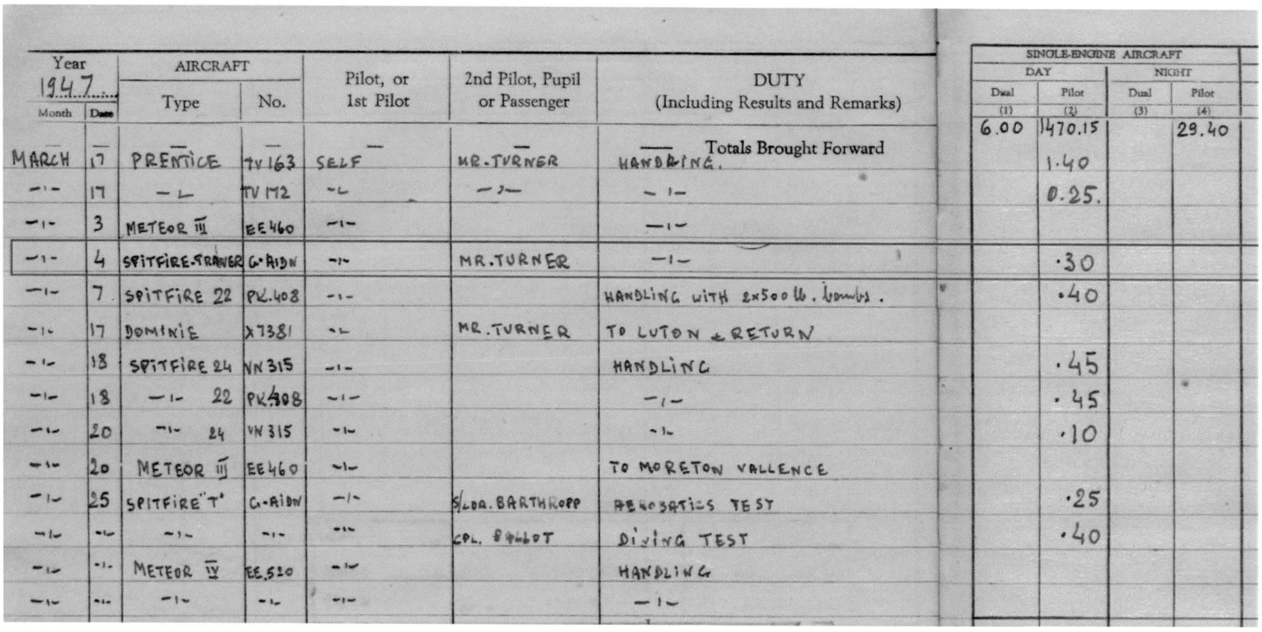

Year 1947 Month	Date	AIRCRAFT Type	No.	Pilot, or 1st Pilot	2nd Pilot, Pupil or Passenger	DUTY (Including Results and Remarks)	SINGLE-ENGINE AIRCRAFT DAY Dual (1)	DAY Pilot (2)	NIGHT Dual (3)	NIGHT Pilot (4)
—	—	—	—	—	—	Totals Brought Forward	6.00	1470.15		29.40
MARCH	17	PRENTICE	TV 163	SELF	MR. TURNER	HANDLING.		1.40		
-"-	17	-"-	TV 172	-"-	-"-	-"-		0.25.		
-"-	3	METEOR III	EE 460	-"-		-"-				
-"-	4	SPITFIRE TRAINER	G-AIDN	-"-	MR. TURNER	-"-		·30		
-"-	7	SPITFIRE 22	PK.408	-"-		HANDLING WITH 2×500 lb. bombs.		·40		
-"-	17	DOMINIE	X7381	-"-	MR. TURNER	TO LUTON & RETURN				
-"-	18	SPITFIRE 24	VN 315	-"-		HANDLING		·45		
-"-	18	-"- 22	PK.408	-"-		-"-		·45		
-"-	20	-"- 24	VN 315	-"-		-"-		·10		
-"-	20	METEOR III	EE 460	-"-		TO MORETON VALLENCE				
-"-	25	SPITFIRE "T"	G-AIDN	-"-	S/LDR. BARTHROPP	AEROBATICS TEST		·25		
-"-	-"-	-"-	-"-	-"-	CPL. ELLIOT	DIVING TEST		·40		
-"-	-"-	METEOR IV	EE.520	-"-		HANDLING				
-"-	-"-	-"-	-"-	-"-		-"-				

MT818 suffered a wheels-up landing on 18 September 1948 and was subsequently repaired by Vickers at Chilbolton. Below is an extract from the Vickers report detailing the repair work undertaken.

TELEPHONE: CHANDLERS FORD - 2251   TELEGRAMS: SUPERMARIN, WINCHESTER

Vickers-Armstrongs Limited.
(AIRCRAFT SECTION)

SUPERMARINE WORKS
~~HURSLEY PARK,~~
~~WINCHESTER, HANTS.~~

Report No.

G-AIDN/HLB/REPAIR/1.

11th November 1948.

YOUR REF.   Chilbolton Aerodrome,
OUR REF.   Nr. Stockbridge.

Final Report on the work carried out to
repair Spitfire Trainer G-AIDN after the
wheels up landing of 18. 9. 48.

The following work repairs and replacements have been carried out:

1. Sample datum longeron bolts removed for examination and refitted. Satisfactory.

2. Sample wing root attachments bolts (top and bottom, port and starboard). Removed for examination and refitted. Satisfactory.

3. Fuselage structure especially in the fuel tank bay and shell plating examined for distortion or fractures. Satisfactory.

4. Main planes, structure and plating, examined for wrinkles or fracture. Satisfactory.

5. Radiators pressure tested for leaks and found satisfactory.

6. Undercarriage, main and tail oleos removed, pintles and bushes examined for damage or scores. Satisfactory.

(Image extract kindly provided by Richard Paver)

MJ627

As outlined in the chapter dedicated to MJ627 earlier in the book, you will have read that she was assigned to 441 (Silver Fox) Sqn. RCAF and allocated the codes *9G-Q*. During her time with the squadron whilst being flown by P/O Sid Bregman on 27 September 1944 they encountered and engaged a lone Bf109 managing to force it down.

This encounter is recorded, and highlighted for clarity, within the following extract from P/O Bregman's logbook.

YEAR 1944		AIRCRAFT		PILOT, OR 1ST PILOT	2ND PILOT, PUPIL OR PASSENGER	DUTY (INCLUDING RESULTS AND REMARKS)	SINGLE-ENGINE AIRCRAFT				MULTI-ENGINE AIRCRAFT					PASS-ENGER	INSTR/CLOUD FLYING		LINK TRAINER
MONTH	DATE	Type	No.				DAY Dual	DAY Pilot	NIGHT Dual	NIGHT Pilot	DAY Dual	DAY 1st Pilot	NIGHT 2nd Pilot	NIGHT Dual	NIGHT 1st Pilot	NIGHT 2nd Pilot		Dual	Pilot	
						TOTALS BROUGHT FORWARD														
					Summary for August 1944	Spitfire II s	33:40													
						Spitfire V	:30													
				Unit 441 Squadron	Total Spitfire	121:25	4:50												
					Date Aug 31 1944	Operational for Aug.	30:50													
					Signature ABregman	Total Ops.	54:05													
Sept	2	Spitfire II	9G-Q	Self		B19 to B40		:40												
"	3	"	" P	"		Patrol		1:10												
"	5	"	" Q	"		B40 to B52		:30												
"	6	"	" Q	"		Cannon Test: Dieppe		1:00												
"	8	"	" S	"		Patrol		1:45												
"	9	"	" Q	"		Armed Recce		1:10												
"	26	"	" M	"		Air Test		:40												
"	26	"	" Q	"		Patrol NIJMEGEN		1:40			No Huns sighted										
"	26	"	" Q	"		Patrol NIJMEGEN		2:05			Huns Sighted + chased + damaged by w/t Eagle										
"	27	"	" Q	"		Patrol ARNHEM		1:55			1 109E Destroyed + others destroyed by Elphone + 2 Planes										
"	27	"	" P	"		Patrol ARNHEM		1:40			No Huns sighted										
"	28	"	" Q	"		Patrol NIJMEGEN - VENLOM		1:40			No Huns Sighted										
"	29	"	" Q	"		Armed Recce-		1:10			Utrecht - Amersfoort - Uneventful										
"	30	"	" Q	"		Patrol		2:00			Uneventful- One 262 sighted- fired but no hits observed										
"	30	"	" Q	"		B70 to Hawkinge		1:15												
				GRAND TOTAL [Cols. (1) to (10)] 654 Hrs. 55 Mins.		TOTALS CARRIED FORWARD														

(Logbook extract image kindly provided by Richard Paver)

Right: In addition to the logbook entry, the kill was also captured by the on-board gun camera. These are the images from that encounter showing the Bf109 taking fire and billowing smoke.

(Gun camera image kindly provided by Peter Monk)

MJ772

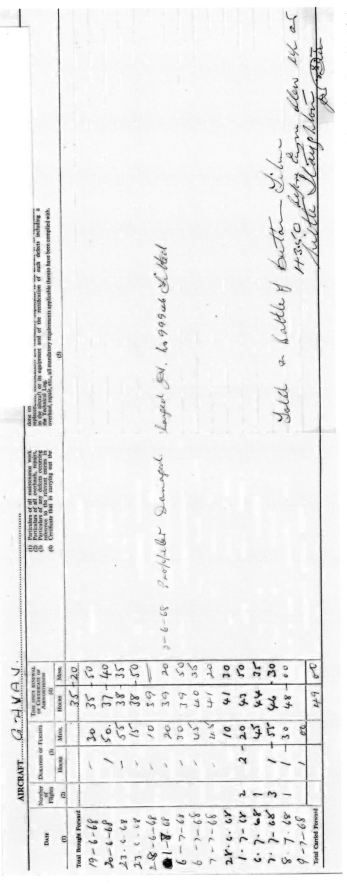

As you will have read the MJ772 chapter earlier in the book you will already know that she was used in the filming of the movie *The Battle of Britain*.

This extract from her logbook records this period, along with the unfortunate forced landing at Little Staughton MJ772 suffered on 9 July 1968. Note the handwritten comment *"Total on Battle of Britain Film 43.50 - Before engine blew up at Little Staughton"*

(Logbook extract kindly provided by Peter Monk)

Modelling the Spitfire Trainer

It has become apparent during our research that there is a huge demand for model Spitfire Trainers, however this is supported by very few suppliers. This disparity has therefore led to high prices for the two-seat Spitfire Trainer models that are available.

For example, a hand-made mahogany 1/22 scale model of the *Boultbee Flight Academy's* Spitfire Mk.IX Trainer SM520 will cost you £495.00!

There are, however, several model kits along with conversion kits available for those looking to create their own Spitfire Trainer. Among these are AZ models who produce a kit in 1/72 scale, and Brigade Models who produce conversion kits in both 1/72 and 1/48 scales.

Left & below: Two views of a 1/32 scale custom modified model of PV202 by Dean Large. The model incorporates many bespoke parts, including canopies. A true work of art!
(Images: Dean Large)

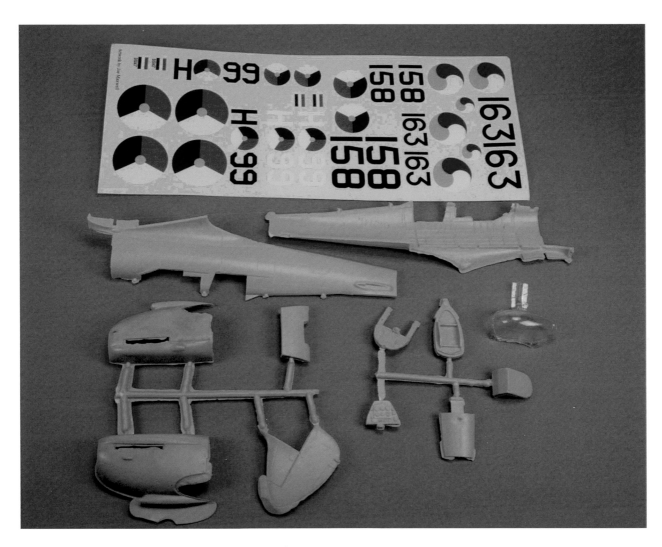

The Brigade Models 1/48 scale Spitfire Trainer conversion kit. *(Image: Dean Large)*

1/72 scale Spitfire Mk.IX Trainer NH341 by Dean Large. *(Image: Dean Large)*

The Art of Aerial Photography – by Richard Paver

I was delighted to be asked by the authors to be the aerial photography consultant for this book. It was a little later that I was then asked to provide an insight of the planning and shooting process that went in to achieve the cover image of three airworthy Spitfire Trainers from the *Biggin Hill Heritage Hangar* (BHHH).

For any air-to-air photography shoot, especially one that involves multiple aircraft, there is a requirement for significant advance planning. There are many variables that go into creating a successful air-to-air shoot, but the number one priority is safety. When the restoration of MJ772 completed in early 2019 the team at BHHH now had three airworthy Spitfire Trainers, and they were very keen to capture some unique images of them all in formation. The last time three or more Spitfire Trainers flew together was with the Irish Air Corps and the Indian Air Force during the 1950s.

The camera-ship chosen for the shoot was the Gipps Aero GA8 Airvan, which had the speed compatibility to safely fly in formations with the Spitfires. The Airvan is extensively used by BHHH as part of their customer Spitfire experiences. The Airvan is a high-wing monoplane very suitable for photography and incorporates an opening window on the Port (left) side along with being able to fly with the sliding door open. The pilots for the shoot were all highly experienced with both the Spitfire and also close formation photographic sorties. The pilots for the sortie were Don Sigourney (MJ772), Dan Griffith (MJ627), and Richard Verrall (MT818), with James Wood flying the Airvan camera-ship.

For this shoot I opted to fly with the door open as it provides such a wide unlimited photographic field. Safety is essential, and we therefore established in advance that this could be achieved. I decided to wear a full harness that would be latched to multiple secure mounting points in the structure of the Airvan. Following discussion with the BHHH engineers I opted to use the structural seat mounting points built into the floor of the Airvan, and also to have an additional back-up safety line. This arrangement required careful advance rigging, including the need for me to check my ability to self-release if the aircraft had to be evacuated for any reason. I knew from previous flights in the Airvan that the intercom with the pilot was clear with either the door or window open, and whilst internal wind buffet did occur with the door open it was not at a level to prevent photography.

Above: Richard Paver in a North American T.28 Trojan, on a previous air-to-air shoot. *(Image: Richard Paver)*

Above: The Airvan at Biggin Hill before the air-to-air shoot. Note the open door. *(Image: Richard Paver)*

Medium to high levels of turbulence are a major problem and can prevent securing the right end result. Levels of turbulence depend on the prevailing weather conditions, the flown height, and the speed of the sortie. We therefore agreed that if the turbulence were too high then we would fly the sortie with the door closed and use the window only. Whilst this would mean the field of view would be more restricted, it would still allow some photographs to be achieved on the sortie.

The sortie was planned from a photographic perspective to include individual shots, two-ship formations and finally the primary objective, the three-ship formation. A sequence was agreed for the individual and pairs formation shots to include shooting both sides of the aircraft, which meant shooting through the window glazing on the Starboard (right) side of the Airvan. Before the briefing I checked the shackle positions on the floor of the Airvan to ensure I could close the door and also safely move to the other side of the aircraft with my harness still fully attached. For the main three-ship formation I kept the shooting to the Port side through the opening door, to keep the formation as simple as possible.

I prepared my harnesses and cameras inside the Airvan, double and triple checked just about everything, before carrying out a detailed briefing with all pilots in a conference room at BHHH. A detailed flying brief was led by Richard Verrall and Dan Griffith for all pilots which covered all aspects of the sortie. Then I led a secondary brief to cover the photographic elements, including a list and sequence of photo serials (a military term describing a photo formation within a sortie), formation changes, and the back-up plan should any of the Spitfires become unserviceable. The plan included staggered departure times, with the Airvan launching first and proceeding to the agreed rendezvous (RV) point, followed by the Spitfires.

The pilot in command of the Airvan was James Wood, who would be flying from the left-hand seat. It was also agreed that Joe Hirst from BHHH would be in the right-hand seat as a safety pilot. As an additional safety precaution, it was decided to have a BHHH engineer onboard to ensure nothing fouled my harness or safety lines and to assist with opening and closing of the door in flight.

The camera-ship pilot has an extremely high workload during a photographic sortie as he is responsible for the navigation, smooth formation flying, all formation changes, radio communications, and avoidance of other air traffic and any restricted airspace. The addition of a safety pilot assists greatly with this workload, as well as providing an additional pair of eyes for collision avoidance awareness. The pilot of the camera-ship must also have a clear understanding of the agreed formation changes, along with their photo serial sequence.

During the photography I am at all times conscious of any undesirable backgrounds, such as industrial estates or solar farms, which means the RV point is carefully chosen taking due consideration of these factors.

At the agreed start-up time we strapped in and set off for the agreed RV point. The first Spitfire to follow us was MJ772, piloted by Don Sigourney, who quickly joined us. I proceeded to shoot a short sequence of solo shots of MJ772 from both sides of the Airvan in both left and right-hand turns. Six minutes later, as briefed, Dan Griffith joined us in MJ627, and I took a quick sequence of two-ship formation shots with both Don and Dan taking it turn to lead. Both pilots are hugely experienced in aerial close formation photo work so on my signal they changed the lead smoothly and easily. For safety, and as the aircraft are so close to one another, each component of a formation change involves a single move in one dimension only. This is then followed by other distinct moves for the aircraft to move into its new formation position, which makes the change process clear for everyone to understand and conduct safely.

After a further six minutes the third Spitfire (MT818), with pilot Richard Verrall and passenger Greg Davis, took off from Biggin Hill and joined the formation in the No. 3 position. I had to now work quickly to secure the photograph which was the main objective of the flight. During the briefing I had set the plan for this shot to be taken in a right-hand turn with the Spitfires in echelon formation off the port (left) wing of the Airvan. This formation was chosen so that the subject aircraft are seen turning towards the camera with the sunlight evenly balanced across each aircraft. The camera-ship would lead the formation throughout and maintain a smooth turn at a constant airspeed & altitude with a constant angle of bank. The angle of bank is agreed between me and the camera-ship pilot via the intercom as we start the first turn because I vary it depending upon the conditions.

The challenge was then on for the three Spitfire pilots to maintain position in lumpy turbulence. Prior to take-off we discussed and agreed visual reference points for each pilot so that aircraft in the formation would have uniform spacing and separation in the finished photograph. I am sitting on the floor in the open door shooting with a hand-held primary camera plus a backup. In order to get best use of the time I have to know my equipment instinctively, so that in the event of an equipment failure – thankfully, very rare – I would instantly swap to the backup camera and not try to solve an issue whilst airborne. Key compositional issues to look out for are to avoid sloping horizons and messy backgrounds, get the lighting right, maintain pin-sharpness whilst using a slow shutter speed, and if possible, have the subjects flying into and not out of the photograph. After a couple of 360° orbits, I confirmed that the whole team had been successful. This was thanks to the high level of formation flying skills demonstrated by all four pilots which made my job a lot easier.

I then called for Richard Verrall in Spitfire No. 3 (MT818) to break and return to base, who was then followed by Don Sigourney in MJ772. We stayed with Dan Griffith in MJ627 for a short solo shoot which included two break shots.

On return to Biggin Hill, having safely taxied back and shut down, the first shout was to "put the kettle on". It was tea all round and a short debrief to share any lessons learned and issues arising.

The photograph was released by BHHH to coincide with their announcement in May 2019 that another Spitfire Trainer (TE308) was on the way from the USA to join the collection. Hopefully, the next time we do this we will have four Spitfire Trainers up!

RAF Repair Categories

Throughout this book we have mentioned various damage classifications, e.g. Cat.Ac. These repair categories are official Air Ministry designations as set out in Air Publications S.154, and we provide the full definitions here for reference.

Between 1941 and 1952 the categories were as follows,

Category	Definition
Cat. U	Aircraft undamaged.
Cat. A	Aircraft can be repaired by unit. (first/front line).
Cat. Ac	Repair is beyond unit capacity. May be repaired on site by another unit or a contractor. (second line).
Cat. B	Beyond repair on site. Repairable at a Maintenance Unit or at a contractor's works. (third line).
Cat. C	Allocated to Instructional Airframe duties (for ground training).
Cat. E	Un-repairable: Aircraft is a write-off (struck off charge). Scrap.
Cat. E1	Aircraft is a write-off but considered suitable for component recovery.
Cat. E2	Aircraft is a write-off and suitable only for scrap.
Cat. E3	Aircraft is burnt out.
Cat. Em	Missing from an operational sortie. (missing aircraft categorised 'Em' after 28 days).

In addition to the above the cause of the damage was sometimes indicated as a prefix or suffix, as follows:

Prefix/Suffix	Definition
EA	Enemy Action
FA	Flying Accident
FB	Flying Battle
GA	Ground Accident
T	Technical Cause

GLOSSARY

Term	Definition
A&AEE	Aeroplane and Armament Experimental Establishment, Boscombe Down
AFS	Advanced Flying School
ALG	Advanced Landing Ground
AOC	Air Officer Commanding
ARF	Aircraft Repair Flight
AST	Air Service Training
BAe	British Aerospace Ltd.
Bf	Prefix for Messerschmitt aircraft type numbers (Bayerische Flugzeugwerke)
Capt.	Captain
Cat	Category (of accident)
Cne.	Captaine (French Air Force)
Circus	Codename for large formation of fighters escorting bombers to bring enemy fighters into combat
DFC	Distinguished Flying Cross
DSO	Distinguished Service Order
FG	Fighter Group
F/O	Flying Officer
Flt. Lt.	Flight Lieutenant
Fw	Prefix for Focke Wulf aircraft type numbers
GSU	Group Support Unit
IAC	Irish Air Corps
IAF	Italian Air Force
Lt.	Lieutenant
Mk.	Mark
MU	Maintenance Unit
NZ	New Zealand
OTU	Operational Training Unit
P/O	Pilot Officer
PoW	Prisoner of War
RAF	Royal Air Force
Ramrod	Codename for large formation of fighters escorting bombers with the intention of destroying a target
RCAF	Royal Canadian Air Force
REAF	Royal Egyptian Air Force
RIAF	Royal Indian Air Force
RNAS	Royal Naval Air Station
RNethAF	Royal Netherlands Air Force
Rodeo	Codename for fighter sweep with bombers
RSU	Repair and Salvage Unit
SAAF	South African Air Force
Sgt.	Sergeant
SOC	Struck off Charge
SoTT	School of Technical Training
Sqn.	Squadron
Sqn. Ldr.	Squadron Leader
Sweep	Fighter operations over enemy territory
2nd TAF	Second Tactical Air Force
UK	United Kingdom
USA	United States of America
USAAF	United States Army Air Force
Wg. Cdr.	Wing Commander
W/O	Warrant Officer

BIBLIOGRAPHY

Books

2nd TAF Spitfire (The Story of Spitfire ML407)	H. Smallwood, British Aviation Heritage, 1986
Dutch Spitfires (Part 1 – History Details)	H. Van Der Meer. Airnieuws Nederland, 1986
Dutch Spitfires (Part 2 – A Technical Study)	H. Van Der Meer & T. Melchers, Repro Holland, 1988
Red Stars Vol.4 (Lend-lease Aircraft in Russia)	C-F. Geust & G. Petrov, Apali Oy, 2002
Spitfire Elizabeth and the Roaring Boys	N. Oram, Grosvenor House Publishing, 2019
Spitfire International	H. Terbeck, H. Van der Meer & R. Sturtivant. Air Britain, 2002
Spitfires in the Sun	V. Singh. Ambi Knowledge Resources, 2014
Spitfire Mk.IX in the Israeli Air Force Service	A.Yofe, White Crow Publications, 2005
Spitfire. The History	E. Morgan & E. Shacklady. Key Books, 2000
Spitfire. The Story of a Famous Fighter	B. Robertson, Harleyford Publications, 1960
Spitfire Singh	M. Edwards, Bloomsbury Publishing India, 2016
Spitfire Survivors (Volume 1)	G. Riley, P.R. Arnold & G. Trant. A-Eleven Publications, 2010
Supermarine Aircraft since 1914	C.F. Andrews & E.B. Morgan. Putnam & Company, 1981
The Irish Air Corps (An Illustrated Guide)	J. Maxwell & P.J Cummins. Max Decals Publ, 2009
The Spitfire in South African Air Force Service	S. McLean, GR Printing and Publishing, 2001
The Spitfire Story	A. Price. Silverdale Books, 2002
The Supermarine Spitfire Part 1 (Merlin)	R.A. Franks. Valiant Wings Publishing, 2018
Wings of Fame, The Journal of Classic Combat Aircraft (Vol.9)	Aerospace Publishing, 1997

Web Resources

Aero Legends	www.aerolegends.co.uk
Aircraft Restoration Company	www.aircraftrestorationcompany.com
Boultbee Flight Academy	www.boultbeeflightacademy.co.uk
Classic Wings	www.classicwings.co.uk
Fly A Spitfire (Biggin Hill Heritage Hangar)	www.flyaspitfire.com
Ultimate Warbird Flights (Air Leasing)	www.ultimatewarbirdflights.com
Warbird Adventure Rides	www.warbird.co.nz

Aviation-Safety.net	www.aviation-safety.net
Dutch Registration	www.strijdbewijs.nl/birds/spitfire/registraties.htm
Geoff Goodall - Warbirds Directory (Supermarine)	www.goodall.com.au/warbirds-directory-v6/vickerssupermarine.pdf
Go Action Stations	www.goactionstations.co.uk
National Archives	www.discovery.nationalarchives.gov.uk
Somme Aviation	www.somme-aviation-39-45.fr
Wings Museum	www.wingsmuseum.co.uk/spitfire_ix_bs548_france.htm

Autumnal silhouette. A stunning image of Spitfire Mk.IX Trainer PV202 operated by *Aerial Collective*, captured on 30 September 2018 at Duxford Airfield in Cambridgeshire. *(Image: Peter Green)*

...and finally!

We hope that you have enjoyed our book. Our goal was to produce a single volume encompassing the entire story of this lesser-known, and rare, Spitfire Trainer variant from inception through to today, and we think this has been achieved.

We also dearly hope that the aircraft histories, the wonderful accompanying photographs, and the accounts of actually flying in these magnificent machines has encouraged and inspired you to take flight yourself in the most beautiful and elegant aircraft of all time, namely "The Spitfire".

THE AUTHORS

Greg Davis is best known in the Spitfire world as the founder of *The Two-Seat Spitfire Page* on Facebook. Since its inception in 2016, the page has become the go-to place for news and views relating to passenger flights in Spitfires. Greg is the author of The Two-Seat Spitfires and, having flown in most of the Vickers-style two-seat Spitfires, he regularly speaks at events on this subject.

John Sanderson is a Spitfire expert and historian. Renowned for his knowledge of the world's surviving Spitfire population, John has written about the topic on many occasions, as well as providing his expertise to several publications in both the UK and around the world. Most notably John was a consultant on the seminal work *Spitfire Survivors*. He has spent many years getting his hands dirty working with historic aircraft, predominantly Spitfires. Greg invited John to join in the endeavour to create the most comprehensive work on the Spitfire Trainer ever written.

Peter Arnold should not need an introduction to anyone who knows about the Spitfire. He is probably best known for his gathering and rebuilding of his Seafire Mk.46 and Spitfire Mk.XII, but also as the co-author of the definitive work *Spitfire Survivors*, a 1000+ page two volume tour-de-force publication detailing the history of every surviving Spitfire and Seafire across the world. Peter has spent a lifetime traveling to well over 120 countries tracking down and photographing Spitfires. He has amassed a world class collection with something in the region of excess of 100k photographs along with hundreds of important historical documents. His research has enabled many previously unidentified Spitfires around the world to reveal their true RAF serial identity. He still has a Mk.22 Spitfire project tucked away in his workshop. Greg and John invited Peter to join the project to allow the 'Complete Story' to be told.

A fine study of Prototype Spitfire Trainer Mk. VIII MT818 over the Kentish countryside in the hands of pilot Richard Verrall, 1 July 2016. *(Image: Richard Paver)*

WS - #0109 - 111220 - C128 - 297/210/14 - CC - 9781784567255 - Gloss Lamination